3647

PHOENIX F
13613
Phoenix, AZ 85022

Like the facets of a diamond
—each side of the cut gem
contributing to its brilliance—
studies about Christ reveal
his many-sided personality.
To the sorrowing, he brings
comfort; to the fearful, courage;
to the weak, strength; to the
hungry, the bread of life;
to the thirsty, living water,
and to the repentant sinner,
salvation.
In this book, the author brings
his readers face to face with
the many-faceted Christ, depicting him as "revolutionary,"
"unconquerable," "compas-
sionate," "powerful," "praying,"
and perhaps most important
of all—"living." Readers of this
book can not help being
challenged by the Christ who
promised *"that they (men)
might have life, and that they
might have it more abundantly
(John 10:10).*

Library
Oakland S.U.M.

JESUS THE REVOLUTIONARY

BY H. S. VIGEVENO

PHOENIX FIRST PASTORS COLLEGE
13613 N. Cave Creek Rd.
Phoenix, AZ 85022

A Division of G/L Publications
Glendale, California, U.S.A.

Over 90,000 in print
Second Printing, 1967
Third Printing, 1968
Fourth Printing, 1970
Fifth Printing, 1971

© Copyright 1966 by G/L Publications
All rights reserved
Printed in U.S.A.

Published by
Regal Book Division, G/L Publications
Glendale, California 91209 U.S.A.

ISBN 0-8307-0012-9

IN APPRECIATION

My thanks to the publishers
who allowed the use of the
quotations included in
Jesus The Revolutionary.
My deep appreciation also
to Miss Margaret Echard for
her encouragements to write:
To Miss Avis Murley for her
diligent preparation of
the manuscript;
And not least, to my wife for
her helpful comments
and suggestions.

H. S. Vigeveno

CONTENTS

CHAPTER 1

THE REVOLUTIONARY JESUS

"Never man spake
like this man" (John 7:46)

In the year 53 A.D. a forceful little man of un-paralleled devotion came to the capital of a great nation. This nation had flourished. She had given to the world the finest human reasoning, the most profound philosophies, great art, architecture, literature and drama. Greece was the most advanced of all cultures. But the Apostle Paul saw in Athens an inadequate foundation beneath this flourishing civilization.

"Ye men of Athens . . . I beheld your devotions, and I found an altar with this inscription, TO THE UNKNOWN GOD."[1] God the Unknown—not sufficient to build upon. God the Known—this alone would suffice. "Whom therefore ye ignorantly worship, Him declare I unto you." Paul proclaimed Christ, the revelation of God, who had lived and died and risen from the dead. Some laughed. A few were willing to investigate further. But this had to be said.

Greece with all its accomplishments had built on

---

[1] Acts 17:22,23

God, the Unknown. Greece as an empire was finished. And Christianity with God revealed in Jesus Christ was the new and adequate and only faith. From the unknown to the known. The truth must be proclaimed. Better shatter a dream than conceal the truth!

Years ago men looked at the heavens. They saw the sun rise in the morning, set in the evening. They saw the moon and stars move in the dark above. And they concluded that the earth was the center of the universe, that all luminaries revolved about it. Then came men of science. Their discoveries led them to believe that it was exactly the other way around. The earth moved about the sun. They were laughed at. They were scorned. But they had to tell the truth. Better shatter a dream than conceal the truth.

A famous 17th century painting hung in a museum. For years the museum authorities had wanted to have the old master cleaned, but they deliberated a long time since the painting was so valuable. When the specialists did proceed they noticed to their great consternation that specks of paint came off in the process. They proceeded with greater care, but could not keep the paint from disintegrating. As they finished the job they discovered another painting beneath. A later artist had tried to improve the original masterpiece. Now they saw the truth. Better shatter a dream than conceal the truth.

I am about to shatter a dream . . . a dream which has grown up through the centuries . . . a dream portrait of Jesus that many hands have touched. The original portrait is in the gospels, but many have tried to improve the original and thereby have spoiled it. By trying to make Jesus more attractive, they have made Him unattractive. By trying to make Him more appealing, they have lost His divine appeal. It may hurt to shatter a dream. But, better shatter a dream than conceal the truth.

Take the commercial art, the almost obnoxious, sentimentally-sweet commercial art, from which we get our impressions of Jesus. He looks like a religious weakling. A soft, somewhat emaciated, ethereal, even effeminate creature seems to ask for our pity, rather than demand our devotion. His complexion is pasty. His cheeks are faintly tinted. His mouth is prettily rouged. His curly, golden hair flows girlishly over His shoulders. And His long, flowing robes place Him in the long ago and far away. He does not smile. He does not speak. He does not demand. *He does nothing!* The pictures are purely sentimental.

Peter Marshall cried out: "We have had enough of the emaciated Christ, the pale, anemic, namby-pamby Jesus, the 'gentle Jesus, meek and mild.' Perhaps we have had too much of it. Let us see the Christ of the gospels, striding up and down the dusty miles of Palestine, sun-tanned, bronzed, fearless."[2]

Clean the canvas. Get back to the original. Not this religious weakling of our imagination. Not this affected emotionalist of our pretty pictures. But the Christ commanding in His manner, challenging in His message, conquering in His manhood, compelling in His mission—the revolutionary Christ! It may

[2]Catherine Marshall, "A Man Called Peter", McGraw-Hill, p. 301

hurt to shatter the dream, but shatter it we must to see the true Master. Better shatter a dream than conceal the truth.

Surely this was no weak affected religionist who walked the shores of Galilee and called to rough fishermen, "Follow Me." His very manner carried authority and purpose. They left their nets to follow this commander of men.

Or, how can you escape the revolutionary manner with which He handled Himself in His hometown? He had started His preaching tour of Galilee and returned to Nazareth. His fame preceded Him, and when He entered the synagogue on the Sabbath Day they asked Him to say a few words. He took the scroll of Isaiah and read:

"The Spirit of the Lord is upon me,

Because he anointed me to preach good tidings to the poor,

He hath sent me to proclaim release to the captives,

And recovering of sight to the blind,

To set at liberty them that are bruised,

To proclaim the acceptable year of the Lord."[3]

He returned the scroll and said: "This very day this Scripture has been fulfilled . . . I expect you will be saying this proverb to me, 'Cure yourself, doctor!' Let us see you do in your country all that we have heard that you did in Capernaum. I assure you that no prophet is ever welcomed in his own country."[4]

They were beside themselves. What right had He to accuse them? Who was He, the carpenter . . .

[3]Lk. 4:18-19
[4]Lk. 4:20-26 Phillips

5

Joseph's son? They rose up as one man, an angry mob. They took Him from the synagogue, through the village, out the road that led to the cliff, to the very edge. They were about to rush Him, throw Him over. He stood there piercing them with His eyes, then walked toward them. They parted as the Red Sea for the children of Israel, and He walked through the midst of the whole lynch-minded mob. Revolutionary is His manner!

True, He was so approachable that children drew near to Him and little ones nestled in His arms, yet so austere that demons cried out in terror in His presence. He was so humble that He washed the disciples' feet, yet so commanding in the temple that the hucksters and traders fell all over each other trying to get away from the fire in His eyes. These are the contrasts in Jesus.

We have seen Him with a sheep in His arms, tender and kind, but failed to see Him, face aflame with the holiness of God. Pascal "sought to rediscover Christianity in its original form, distinguishing it clearly from its later contact with the mentality of the West."[5] So we must rediscover this Christ, so revolutionary in His manner.

His message is far more than a pleasant homily on the golden rule. He interpreted His message with a quotation from the Old Testament referring to Himself as a "stone." This stone is offensive. This stone lies in our path. We may stumble over it. We must reckon with it.

Even such a deceptively mild statement as, "Con-

[5]Quoted from Emile Cailliet, "Pascal, The Emergence of Genius," Harper, p. 291-292

sider how the lilies grow in the fields; they do not work, they do not spin; and yet, I tell you, even Solomon in all his splendour was not attired like one of these,"[6] is like a stone of stumbling. To us the epitome of life may be to loll about in luxury by the side of our own swimming pool, or to go nightclub-bing in the most fashionable furs, bedecked with sparkling jewelry. Revolutionary, indeed, to be told that "even Solomon in all his splendour was not attired like one of these." How changed all our values would be if we could see it that way.

Or, what of Jesus' authoritative declaration: "The Son of man is Lord even of the sabbath day?"[7] We consider ourselves masters of our own time, and if not our work week, at least masters of that one day in seven for leisure. It is our Sunday to do with as we choose. Why should we let Him be "Lord of the sabbath day?" How changed our Sundays would be if we heeded His revolutionary message. But then, that is a stone we stumble over, too.

What most agitated the good people of His day was the manner in which Jesus took on Himself the prerogatives of God. "My son, your sins are forgiven."

And they said: "Why does the fellow talk like that? This is blasphemy! Who but God alone can forgive sins?"[8]

This stone lies in our path also since we are slow to accept forgiveness. "I must be worthy," we say; "I must be good enough to be forgiven." And so with a

[6]Mt. 6:28,29 English
[7]Mt. 12:18
[8]Mk. 2:5-7 English

perverted sense of guilt we strap these sins to ourselves. We want to punish ourselves, because we feel we deserve it. Thereby we nullify the gospel of forgiveness. "Your sins *are* forgiven." Jesus has power to forgive sins.

The people who heard Him began to draw conclusions. "When Christ cometh, will He do more miracles than these which this man hath done? This is the Christ. This is the Prophet."[9] The religious leaders found it necessary to take action against Him and sent the temple police to arrest Him. These officers were to mingle with the crowd and wait for some opportune moment, some word for which they could take Him. The religious leaders convened, but the officers returned empty-handed.

"Why have ye not brought him?" they asked.

"Never man spake like this man," they answered.

"What?" they said, "have any of the rulers of the Pharisees believed on him? But this people who knoweth not the law are cursed."[10] What an unconscious compliment to the revolutionary message of Jesus: "Never man spake like this man."

Behind the message is the Man. "The most important thing about a sermon," declares Joseph Parker, "is the man behind it." Not always true, but in the case of Jesus, yes. "Manhood is the best sermon," says Henry Ward Beecher.[11]

What a Man He must have been to endure not only the cruelties of the Cross, but even the tiring,

[9]Jn. 7:31,40,41
[10]Jn. 7:45-49
[11]Quoted from Ian Macpherson, "The Burden of the Lord," Abingdon, p. 45

demanding years of service to humanity. He could never have lived the rugged life He lived had He not been physically equipped. A carpenter in those days did not buy his wood wholesale, but went out, chose his young tree, swung his axe and brought the wood home himself. And He had been doing that for a dozen years before He began His wearisome travels (on foot), His untiring ministry.

But more than His physical appearance, do we grasp what Jesus claimed for Himself as a man? He took the great of the past and put Himself above them—an act of impertinent arrogance, or else there is something revolutionary about His manhood.

They asked: "Are you greater than our father Abraham?"

He answered: "Before Abraham was born, I am."[12]

The woman of Samaria asked: "Are you a greater man than Jacob our ancestor, who gave us this well?"

He answered: "Everyone who drinks this water will be thirsty again, but whoever drinks the water that I shall give him will never suffer thirst any more."[13]

They said: "Our ancestors had manna to eat in the desert; as Scripture says, 'He gave them bread from heaven to eat.' "

Jesus said: "The truth is, not that Moses gave you the bread from heaven, but that my Father gives you

[12]Jn. 8:53,58 English
[13]Jn. 4:12-14 English

the real bread from heaven. I am the bread of life. I have come down from heaven."[14]

They asked: "Are you greater than . . . the prophets?"

He answered: "I have come . . . to complete . . . the prophets. I am the Son of God."[15]

And if Solomon was the wisest of them all, He claimed: "The queen of the south . . . came from the uttermost parts of the earth to hear the wisdom of Solomon; and, behold, a greater than Solomon is here."[16]

Greater than Abraham, Jacob, Moses, Solomon, the prophets is this revolutionary man, Jesus . . . commanding in His manner, challenging in His message, conquering in His manhood, compelling in His mission.

Kingdoms have come and gone. Armies marched and retreated. Empires flourished and decayed, but Jesus has the audacity to affirm that His kingdom is eternal, that His mission cannot be thwarted: "I will build My Church, and the gates of hell shall not prevail against it."[17]

"O where are kings and empires now
    Of old that went and came?
But, Lord, Thy Church is praying yet,
    A thousand years the same."

Our world has witnessed many a revolution, but none as effective as the one that divided history into B.C. and A.D. Every revolution involves the shedding

[14]Jn. 6:31-38 English
[15]Jn. 8:53, 10:36; Mt. 5:17 Phillips
[16]Mt. 12:42
[17]Mt. 16:18

of blood. So did this one. Not as much blood, perhaps, but the quality of the One far outweighs the quantity of others. Revolutionary, indeed, this mission, to begin with a cross and sway the whole world through suffering love. Revolutionary to build a Church on the sacrifice that offers man forgiveness and atonement with God.

More—the heart of the mission is Jesus Himself. In heaven as on earth all depends on how we respond to Him. He dares to say: "Whosoever therefore shall confess Me before men, him will I confess also before My Father who is in heaven. But whosoever shall deny Me before men, him will I also deny before My Father who is in heaven."[18] This is why He has come to earth, to be our Saviour, to bring us to God, to establish the Church, to become our Judge.

Among the many artists who have tried to represent Jesus Christ, few have captured this revolutionary aspect like Michelangelo. In the Sistine Chapel in Rome, Michelangelo has painted "The Last Judgment", depicting the risen Christ who divides mankind: "Whosoever therefore shall confess Me . . . whosoever shall deny Me . . ." One can see the strength of Jesus revealed in that massive torso, not covered by any robes, that magnificent, massive torso . . . muscles bulging, every muscle in action. His arm is uplifted in judgment, yet one hand shows a certain gentleness. The head, almost a little small for the handsome physique, is held upright by a powerful neck . . . His jaw set, mouth firm, eyes

[18]Mt. 10:32,33

11

looking straight down in divine justice—face full of emotion—He *is* the Judge.

And yet the spear-wound in His side, the nail-prints in His hands, are clearly visible, and that face expresses suffering love. Mercy and justice have kissed each other!

I have tried to shatter a dream. A dream of the gentle Jesus, meek and mild so often superimposed on the Christ of the gospels. He is Lord and Christ who entered this world in a revolutionary manner with a revolutionary message. "Never man spake like this man." A revolutionary man with a revolutionary mission.

So God does not merely speak to us from the remote regions of heaven, but in Jesus Christ comes down into our world and calls us to revolution: "I will build my Church." I want you in it. I want you a part of it . . . A new life. A new relationship with God, the Father. Love. Forgiveness. Joy. Peace. A revolution indeed:

"If a man is in Christ he becomes a new person altogether—the past is finished and gone, everything has become fresh and new."[19]

---

[19]2 Cor. 5:17 Phillips

CHAPTER 2

THE UNCONQUERABLE JESUS

"Then the devil leaveth him . . ."
(Mt. 4:11)

Amazing, isn't it, that we are still talking about Jesus? After two thousand years people meet in almost every conceivable spot on earth to worship Jesus Christ. Books dot our libraries; art adorns our galleries; and reams of music are all about Him. Like a majestic mountain-peak towering over a landscape, the unconquerable Christ stands today. Forces have been arrayed against Him. Foes have encountered Him. But He remains unvanquished, undefeated, unconquerable.

This is the portrait I want you to see now in our gallery, the portrait of the unconquerable Christ. During His life He endured opposition. Even then He came forth victorious. All through history He has been attacked. Still He remains unconquerable. Come closer to the canvas. Examine with me some of the details of this portrait of Christ.

When Jesus came forth in response to God's call, after submitting to the baptism of John, He was driven by the Spirit of God into the wilderness. Here He met his first real test. Here He faced an encounter with the Devil. (I am not about to argue the existence of the Devil. Jesus did not argue about his existence. He experienced the temptations. He felt the power of attack. He entered into conversation with the Tempter. This being the case, I do not have to offer proofs, or argue the Devil's existence.)

After forty days and nights of fasting, the Devil came to Him in that wilderness: "If you are the Son of God, tell these stones to become bread."[1] The temptation is not theoretical, theological, or philosophic. It is in His stomach which growls and hurts. And how can a man pray when he feels these pangs of hunger? How can he think of God and commune with God when there is nothing but that empty gnawing in his stomach?

Furthermore, what is wrong with turning stones into bread? If you really are the Son of God, you can do that! You should do it, too! That is your obligation. If you can—feed the whole world! Why not stop the angry outcry of starving millions? Why not put a halt to all the blasphemies of the hungry? Why not prove once and for all that God is love? Feed the world! First begin with yourself. And when you have turned stones into bread, you will have proven to yourself that you really are in God's favor. Then you will know you are fully in God's will.

But Jesus did not have to prove anything to Himself. Knowing Himself to be already in God's will, He answers: "It is written, Man shall not live by bread alone, but by every word that proceedeth out

---

[1]For entire story see Mt. 4:1-11 King James & English

15

of the mouth of God." Thus ends the first round. The Devil goes back to his corner, and Jesus remains unconquered.

The Tempter returns. If Jesus will quote Scripture, he also will take his stand on Scripture. He takes Jesus (perhaps in his imagination) to the temple. He places Jesus on a pinnacle of the temple, high above the people. "If you are the Son of God," he says, "Throw yourself down; for Scripture says, 'He will put his angels in charge of you, and they will support you in their arms, for fear you should strike your foot against a stone.' "

You order. God acts. You jump. God's Word rescues you, and you walk away unharmed before the open-mouthed and wide-eyed crowd. If you are the Son of God, why not prove it to everyone? Why not take God's promises into your own hands? Why not take your stand on Scripture? Why not win the world with one grandiose, gigantic display?

But Jesus knows He must never trifle with faith. He must never take the promises of God and use them for His own gratification. This is what the Tempter wants him to do. He can see it now clearly. The Tempter wants Him to think that God owes Him this deliverance! He has a right to jump. He has a right to expect God's miraculous delivering power. No, He has no such right! "Scripture says again, 'You are not to put the Lord your God to the test.' " The end of round two, and Jesus remains unconquered.

A final time the Devil ventures forth. If that is Jesus' position, then Satan will strike where He can really feel it. Why has Jesus come to earth? Why is

He in the world as God's Son? To bring the Kingdom of God to mankind. To bring all men to the knowledge of God. To lead humanity to salvation.

Does Jesus not yearn for this? Is He not consumed by a burning desire to win the world? Will He not shed tears over the city of Jerusalem? And not for the city only, but for the world? "Again, the devil taketh him up into an exceeding high mountain, and sheweth him all the kingdoms of the world, and the glory of them; and saith unto him, All these things will I give Thee, if Thou wilt fall down and worship me."

Be free of God! Don't you want to be free of God? Don't you believe in yourself? Don't you believe in yourself more than anything else? You may yearn for God, but there is a deeper yearning within you, to be on your own. Be free from any Lord, that is what you really want! "The kingdoms of the world are yours! The world for Jesus Christ!"

Jesus again retreats from the center. He is in God's hands. He is under God's Word. He may shed tears for a wayward world and wish to win men, but only on God's terms: "Begone Satan. It is written, Thou shalt worship the Lord thy God, and Him only shalt thou serve."

The end of round three; the battle is over. The Tempter has lost; and he knows it. The most telling temptations have failed to conquer the Son of God. He is the unconquerable Christ, so the Biblical account closes with these victorious words: "Then the devil leaves Him. . . . "

Jesus began His ministry. Many forces were arrayed against Him. His family did not understand

Him. They came to stop Him from His labors, concerned (as relatives can very well be) over His health. His brothers did not believe in Him. In some measure Jesus must have experienced the truth of His pungent remark: "A man's foes shall be they of his own household."[2]

But it was more than that. Blaise Pascal once said: "I assert that if all men knew what each says of the other, there would not remain four friends alive." Jesus knew. They did not say things behind His back, but to His face. He had been born out of wedlock, and nothing good could come from Nazareth. He was not a devoted teacher of God, but a fun-lover, a glutton, a drunkard. He was really possessed by a demon, and in partnership with the Devil himself.

Jesus was not preserved from such derogatory remarks. All this slander did not subdue Him, did not conquer Him, even when His witness was denied. "We speak that we do know, and testify that we have seen; and ye receive not our witness."[3] What can be more discouraging than to be rejected in your life-work, in your contribution to humanity?

You help a man on the Sabbath. You are attacked for helping him. You encourage a paralytic, tell him that his conscience can be at ease, his sin forgiven, and you are laughed at for "forgiving sins." You heal a blind man, and you barely escape stoning. You give love. You receive hate. You speak truth. You hear lies. You sow mercy. You reap judgment.

[2]Mt. 10:36
[3]Jn. 3:11

18

You bring salvation. You get a Cross. Even your own friend betrays you.

You are handed over to the government. The governor says: "I find in him no fault at all."[4] Still he has you beaten, scourged, and he releases a notorious criminal in your place. Again he says: "I find no fault in him."[5] Then he washes his hands of you, exposes you on a cross, seals you in a tomb, and stations a watch in the cemetery.

Misunderstood, hated, despised, rejected—in three short years evil forces did their work. But they could not conquer the unconquerable. Even death could not hold Him. Christ burst the bonds of death and came forth from the tomb on the third day. His triumph is so radical and so complete, that it is obvious—not friend or foe, not priest or Pharisee, not Judas or Pilate, not life or death, could conquer the unconquerable Christ. A victorious Lord leads His disciples to spread the good news. So Christianity began.

There is more to see in this portrait of the unconquerable Christ. Ever since Biblical times men have tried to conquer Him. Men of thought. Men of philosophy. Men of letters. Men of knowledge. Voltaire made the statement that he would show the world, although it took twelve apostles to establish Christianity, it would take only one to tear it down. The Bible would be an antique, he said, one hundred years after his death. "God is dead," says Nietzsche. "Christianity is through," says Voltaire. The Bible is an antique. Conquer the unconquerable Christ? How

[4] Jn. 18:38
[5] Jn. 19:4

preposterous it all sounds when we are still talking about Jesus today!

Now we have something new to occupy us on the earth. Psychology. For all the ills of men, psychology and psychiatry have the answer. If you are depressed, the psychiatrist will analyze you. If you are disturbed, the psychologist may discover the causes of your disturbance. If you feel guilty, self-understanding will help you overcome such guilt feelings.

Psychology is a noble science, and undoubtedly, many are helped. Analysis can lead to an understanding of yourself, but it cannot lead you to a new relationship with God. As one psychoanalyst has put it, there is a new version of the "Ugly Duckling" story. The ugly duckling never discovers he is a swan. He just undergoes analysis and adjusts.

But this is precisely the responsibility of the Christian faith, to show us what we really are, where we have gone wrong, and how we can renew our relationship with God. Nothing can become a substitute for Christ. Salvation does not come to man apart from the Saviour. Forgiveness does not come without the forgiveness of sin through the Cross. We may attempt by modern means to conquer Christ, that is, to find some way to cure our ills, to bring salvation, to 'redeem' man—but man cannot be redeemed without the Redeemer.

This is true, of course, for any other field as well—science, medicine, economics, education. Professor Emile Cailliet says: "In drawing attention to the character of modern frustration. . . .we may ascertain the true nature of our problems. They all are spiritual problems, that is to say, primarily

.... theological." Then he quotes the eminent psychiatrist, Dr. Carl Jung: "There has not been one (of all my patients over thirty-five) whose problem in the last resort was not that of finding a religious outlook on life."[6] This is why Jesus remains the unconquerable Christ. Only the Saviour of the world can "save" the world.

There is yet another way in which we try to conquer Christ. A more popular way—pleasure. Through diversion, through entertainment, we still our restlessness, we fill our solitude, we escape from ourselves. Why do we have to have a transistor along when we go for a walk? Why do we have to have background music? Why are we constantly banishing boredom through entertainment? We allow ourselves to be pushed around by noise, lights, pictures, stories, laughter, rhythm. We want to laugh. We want to be "sent".

What is really happening to us? We are outer-directed. We are constantly being filled by amusements from the outside. And that means we really become emptier and emptier on the inside. The more impressions have to be made on you from the outside, the less you have to show for yourself from the inside. The more you become an object of entertainment, the less you are an individual, a person. The words of Jesus become more and more true: "Whosoever will save his life shall lose it."[7] In trying to save our lives with amusements and diversions, we only lose them. We end up with nothing.

Only the God who created us can fulfill our deep-

---

[6]Emile Cailliet, "The Christian Approach to Culture," p. 210
[7]Mt. 16:25

est needs. "There is within the soul of man a God-shaped vacuum, and only the God who put it there, can fill it."

We cannot displace our need for God. We cannot resolve our own hungers. To anyone who thirsts to be free, to find fulfillment, to come to God, Jesus says: "If any man thirst, let him come unto Me, and drink."[8] Do not take any substitute drinks, come unto Me!

The world has tried to conquer Christ. When He was here, and since His coming, they have all tried —devil and demons, friend and foe, priest and Pharisee, Judas and Pilate, philosophy and psychology, pleasure-seekers and pleasure-finders.

And you have tried, too! You have tried to conquer your hunger for Jesus, your thirst for the Saviour. You have tried to conquer the unconquerable. You have pushed Him into the outer edges of your existence. You have refused to let Him guide in your decisions. You have stubbornly shoved Him away from your conscience, and said: "Hands off, Christ! Hands off my personal life, my thought life, my sex life. It's none of your business what I do with myself, how I spend my time. It's my life to live, not yours. I'll give you a little time on Sunday. I'll pray when I'm in need. Now that's enough, Christ. That's enough."

But He is still there, isn't He? He refuses to be held at arm's length. He is unconquerable. He claims you through His Cross. He has died for you already. And you cannot change that fact with all your argu-

8Jn. 7:37

22

ments, with all your unbelief, with all your rebellious attitudes.

He keeps coming into your life, doesn't He? He wants to win you back to God. He comes just where you keep saying 'no' to Him. Just once say, "yes"! Open the door a crack. Let Him in. See if He can do anything. See if He can remove your guilt. See if He can control your passion. See if He can regulate your thought. See if He can change your action. He is the unconquerable Christ!

And once He comes into you, He can make *you* unconquerable, too. Unconquerable by all the forces of evil, the foes of life, the fears of this temporal existence. Unconquerable, not because of your ability, but because of His power in you. Unconquerable because He has overcome the world. Unconquerable because He has burst death's bonds and is alive forevermore. Unconquerable because He, the unconquerable One, is in you! "Christ in you, the hope of glory."[9] And it will be true of you, as it was of Jesus, "Then the Devil leaves Him. . . ."

---

[9]Col. 1:27

CHAPTER 3

THE CHALLENGING JESUS

"Can ye drink of the cup
that I drink of?" (Mk. 10:38)

Within every one of us lies the thrill of adventure. We yearn for the bold, the daring. We respond to challenge. We are not made for the common place, nor satisfied with routine. We seek escape from the humdrum. That is why we are constantly "on the go" for excitement. We want adventurous living.

So, great explorers have left their country and kindred, and following in the footsteps of Abraham, set out not knowing where they were going. Once Pizarro, explorer of South America, had to challenge his tired and discouraged companions. Drawing a line in the sand and pointing south where lay unexplored regions, Pizarro said: "On that side are toil, hunger, nakedness, the drenching storm, desertion, and death; on this side are ease and pleasure. Choose, each man, what becomes a brave Castilian. For my part, I go to the south!" His men responded to that challenge and ventured south with him.

Men of science wrestle from nature the secrets of

the universe and help the human race to progress against disease.

Men of philosophy seek truth. They are like the philosopher Lessing who declared that if God came to him offering in His right hand the whole of truth, and in His left hand the search for truth with all the toil and travail and trouble of search, he would choose that. Not the finished product. But the adventure of quest.

Leaders of nations inspire their people to rise up to new frontiers. "Ask not what your country can do for you, but what you can do for your country." And in times of war they call a nation to "blood, sweat, and tears." Men respond to such challenges.

So also, a Man lived in a small country among a seemingly insignificant group of people. But His challenge has leapt the barriers of centuries, pounded on the gates of this world, and boldly dared men to adventurous living and vibrant faith.

"A Word came forth in Galilee,
    A Word like to a star;
    It climbed and rang and blessed and burnt
    Wherever brave hearts are."

And men of faith respond. They turn the world upside down in their zeal.

The portrait of the challenging Christ has about it the marching note, the ring of trumpets, the waving of flags, the bold colors of adventure. Christ challenges us to boldness and daring, to adventure and excitement. He strides into our lives and commands: "Follow Me." His is a trumpet-call, a battle-cry, masterful and mighty: "If any man will come after

Me, let him deny himself, take up his cross, and follow Me."[1]

The challenging Christ presents no rocking-chair religion, no peace-of-mind-pap, no come-in-and-be-saved-and-take-it-easy-from-now-on ideology. No escape from life.

What then is the challenge of Jesus Christ? "Follow Me." "If any man will come after Me, let him deny himself. . . ." "Repent. Believe. The Kingdom of God is at hand."[2] It all has something to do with that kingdom. . . . God's Kingdom.

An earthly kingdom is a territory. The land and country (or countries) which belong to a king form his kingdom. The kingdom of God is "not of this world."[3] And yet the kingdom of God is "among you."[4] The kingdom of God is the rule, the reign, and the sovereignty of God. It is not of this world. It is not an earthly territory, but a spiritual realm. Yet the Kingdom is among us wherever God is Lord, wherever God is supreme in any life. Wherever Jesus is, there is the kingdom!

The challenging Christ invites us *to enter his kingdom*. He challenges us to allow God sovereignty over our lives. He challenges us to take God seriously. He challenges us to enter the spiritual realm where God is Lord, indeed. What a great challenge to accept! A new way of life. A new power for our bungling efforts.

Henry Drummond read a letter to a student gath-

---

[1]Mt. 16:24
[2]Mk. 1:15
[3]Jn. 18:36
[4]Lk. 17:21 English

ering. It was an anonymous letter full of bitterness and hopelessness from a man who had made shipwreck of his life. He signed that letter "Thanatos"— the Greek word for 'death'. Drummond confessed that if ever a man was irretrievably lost, it was the writer of that letter. Two years later Drummond faced that same student gathering. "Remember that letter? Gentlemen, I have in my pocket tonight a letter from 'Thanatos' which he sent me this week, and he says he is a changed man—a new creature in Christ Jesus."

Enter! Accept the challenge of a new life. "Enter by the narrow gate. The gate is wide that leads to perdition; there is plenty of room on the road, and many go that way; but the gate that leads to life is small and the road is narrow, and those who find it are few."[5] This is no mild meandering. The challenge to enter is in violent language. Jesus speaks of men pressing into the kingdom. As men attack a city, we must storm our way into the kingdom. The kingdom is for the desperate. The kingdom is for the earnest, the serious.

Christian has come a long way before he gets to the narrow gate in Bunyan's "Pilgrim's Progress." He knocks on the gate. No answer. He knocks again. Still no answer. He persists. Finally someone asks who is there?

"Here is a poor burdened sinner. I come from the City of Destruction, but am going to Mount Zion, that I may be delivered from the wrath to come."

[5] Mt. 7:13,14 English

The gate opens. As Christian enters, he is suddenly, violently seized by his arm and pulled inside.

"What means that?" asked Christian.

"A little distance from this gate, there is erected a strong castle of which Beelzebub is the captain. From thence both he and they that are with him shoot arrows at them that come up to this gate, if haply they may die before they enter in."

Then said Christian: "I rejoice and tremble."

The long journey, the persistent knocking, the struggle and the danger . . . these are part of entering the kingdom.

How does he enter? What is the requisite? "Here is a poor, burdened sinner. . . ." Jesus has not come to call the self-sufficient, but sinners to repentance. He who humbles himself shall be allowed in. He who comes in sincere confession finds the door flung open.

And this gate into the kingdom, this door through which we enter, what is that? "I am the Door: By Me if any man enter in, he shall be saved," said Jesus.[6] He Himself is the Door. He has opened the way to God. He is the entrance into the kingdom. He has done it on a cross. That is why, when I look upon this portrait of the challenging Christ, I see it painted in deep red, even blood-red hues. "I am the Door: by Me if any man enter in, he shall be saved. . . ." "I am the good shepherd: the good shepherd giveth his life for the sheep."[7]

The Challenging Christ also challenges us *to live for his kingdom.* "If any man will come after Me, let

[6]Jn. 10:9
[7]Jn. 10:9,11

30

him deny himself, take up his cross, and follow Me." "He that loveth father or mother more than Me is not worthy of Me; and he that loveth son or daughter more than Me is not worthy of Me. And he that taketh not his cross, and followeth after Me, is not worthy of Me."[8] No rocking-chair religion this. No arm-chair faith. No escape from life.

Here is life with a sharp edge, with the sword of adventure. "As they were going along the road a man said to him, 'I will follow you wherever you go.' Jesus answered, 'Foxes have their holes, the birds their roosts; but the Son of Man has nowhere to lay his head.'

Yet another said, 'I will follow you, Sir; but let me first say goodbye to my people at home.' To him Jesus said, 'No one who sets his hand to the plough and then keeps looking back is fit for the kingdom of God.' "[9] We revere these sayings of Jesus. But do we realize their impact? Live fully for the kingdom of God. They imply complete commitment and utter abandonment.

How can you live like that? Is it possible in this world? The only way to live for the kingdom is to keep the kingdom of God ever before you, as a goal. Then you know why you are living. Such is the adventure of the Christian life. The ancient command to have no other gods before God is psychologically sound. God is first. "Seek ye first the kingdom of God," said Jesus.[10] "One can never draw God too deep into the flesh," writes Martin Luther.

[8]Mt. 10:37,38
[9]Lk. 9:57-62 English
[10]Mt. 6:33

One can never seek too much for the kingdom of God in this life. For then, and then alone, life takes on meaning!

A German pastor stood by a cellar which had been shattered by a bomb. It happened during an air-raid in the Second World War. Fifty people were killed in that cellar. He looked at the pit now, brooding. A woman came to his side: "My husband died down there. His place was right under the hole. The clean-up squad was unable to find a trace of him. We were there the last time you preached in the church. And here before this pit I want to thank you for preparing him for eternity."[11]

That is why I see in the portrait of the challenging Christ also the color of blue. Blue for eternity; blue for the kingdom of heaven. We live with an eye on the next world. Of course, we know that we can become so heavenly-minded that we are no earthly good. But the greater danger is that we become so earthly minded that we are no good for heaven.

Our world of atheistic existentialism, atheistic communism, atheistic materialism—in which Heidegger speaks of forlornness and Sartre of despair—our world has lost *meaning*. Here Jesus challenges us to live for a heavenly kingdom. He reminds us that we came from God. We belong to God. We will one day go back to God. We are always in God's hands. Our times are in the circle of eternity. Therefore, we are to live in a new relationship to our heavenly Father.

Still there is more. Jesus challenges us *to die for*

---

[11]Thielecke, "The Waiting Father"

his kingdom. To enter. To live. If need be, to die. Such is to be our devotion.

"Then Zebedee's two sons James and John approached him, saying, 'Master, we want you to grant us a special request.'

'What do you want me to do for you?' answered Jesus.

'Give us permission to sit one on each side of you in the glory of your Kingdom!'

'You don't know what you are asking,' Jesus said to them. 'Can you drink the cup I have to drink? Can you go through the baptism I have to bear?'

'Yes, we can,' they replied.

Then Jesus told them, 'You will indeed drink the cup I am drinking.' "[12]

This cup was the cup of death. They, too, would drink it. They, too, would die in service for God. Surely, they did not understand the meaning of the cup. Not then. But Jesus weighed His words.

In one way no one could drink of the cup of Jesus. He alone could die for the sin of man. He alone could qualify as "The Lamb of God." He alone could make atonement and be the Saviour of the world. Even in that same conversation about the cup, He said: "The Son of Man came. . . . to give His life a ransom for many."[13]

But the cup of death we may have to drink, too. The cup of suffering we may be called on to share. The cup which identifies us with Jesus Christ is the cup of hardship and hurt, of persecution and pain, of suffering and shame, of degradation and death! "If

[12]Mk. 10:35-39 Phillips
[13]Mt. 20:28

they have persecuted Me, they will persecute you. The servant is not greater than his lord."[14]

"Can you drink the cup I have to drink?"

We want to share Jesus' cup. But we want the cup of peace, the cup of forgiveness, the cup of salvation. Do we know what we pray for when we affirm, "We can drink of your cup!" This cup identifies us with Him who challenges us to follow. Do we realize what trials go into the making of saints?

God is not had for nothing. The kingdom of God is not cheap. We may speak of free salvation, and grace that is given us, but it is not thrown at us, even as pearls are not thrown before swine.

Jesus told us a story of a pearl merchant. The merchant goes looking for a beauty, a once-in-a-lifetime pearl. Somewhere in an Oriental bazaar he finds it: lustrous, beautiful, perfect. He wants it. And when he hears the price, never betraying his excitement, he makes one swift calculation—it will cost him everything he has. Everything!

His cool, down-to-earth friends, if they could talk with him now, would advise him: "Don't go overboard. You can't have this pearl. The price is too high. Don't be a fool. Don't throw everything away for that pearl!"

But he cannot help himself. He must have it. He sells everything for the pearl of great price. Now this beauty is his! Now this once-in-a-lifetime pearl belongs to him!

"This is what the Kingdom of God is like. . . ." A fabulous pearl—only more. It will cost you everything. God is not had for nothing.

---
[14]Jn. 15:20

34

"If any man will come after Me, let him deny himself, and take up his cross, and follow Me. . ."

"Can you drink the cup I have to drink. . .?"

Enter, live, if need be, die, for the kingdom. But wait a minute! Take one look at the man's face. Is he unhappy that he has sold all his goods? Is he bitter because life has cost him everything? I should say not! A smile is on his lips, a glow on his face, for his mind is not at all on what he has given up; only on what he has gained! He has put everything beneath that pearl. Everything is worth giving for this kingdom. Everything is worth selling for God!

That is why Christians could walk into the jaws of lions. That is why they could sing as they were strapped to the stake, as fire made torches of them. That is why they could say like James Guthrie on the day of his execution, looking from his prison window at the morning sun: "This is the day which the Lord hath made; we will rejoice and be glad in it."[15]

Here then is the challenge to adventurous living: Let God be sovereign in your life! Enter His Kingdom. The challenging Christ dares us to follow Him, to drink of His cup, to live and die for the Kingdom of God.

---

[15] Ps. 118:24

CHAPTER 4

THE COMPASSIONATE JESUS

*"When he saw the multitudes,
he was moved with compassion
on them, because they were . . .
as sheep having no shepherd"
(Mt. 9:36)*

We measure the greatness of a man not by the length of his life, not by the breadth of his influence, nor by the height of his successes, but by the depth of his love and devotion. Are we not instinctively drawn to those who sympathize with us, who care, and understand? We all desire to be loved. We all need sympathy, not sentimentality or even pity, but companionship in our loneliness. Length of days, breadth of influence, success—these are not the standards by which we evaluate men. Those who care for us are the people to whom we are drawn.

See then this portrait of the compassionate Christ. It hangs in a very special place in our exhibit— painted in soft, blended shades, conveying all the mercy, and love, even the innermost feelings of Jesus; and through Jesus, the love of God. Compassion is the capacity to suffer with others, to bear their burdens, and to feel their sorrows.

Look then upon this portrait of the compassionate Christ, and look particularly at the eyes of Jesus. See the divine pity with which He scanned the crowd. See the loving compassion with which He looked on mankind. When He saw them, He was moved to the depths of His being; "When He saw the multitudes, He was moved with compassion. . . . because they were as sheep not having a shepherd."[1]

How does a shepherd *see* his sheep? The shepherd "careth for the sheep . . . calleth his own sheep by name. . . . knoweth his sheep. . . . layeth down his life for the sheep. . . giveth unto them eternal life."[2] The shepherd sees each individual sheep. When only ninety-and-nine out of one hundred are within the fold, the shepherd thinks only of that one which is lost, and goes out into the night, searching, until he finds it. Jesus sees every one in a crowd. Every *one* is important.

Here is the difference between other attempts to help man, and the outlook of Jesus. Socially we may belong to the same service organizations. Politically we may belong to the same party and espouse common views. Economically we may be a part of the same union and agree on improving conditions. Even ecclesiastically we may be herded together into the same denomination. But in every such attempt we count sheep instead of seeing sheep. In numbers we lose the individual. Not so Jesus.

Five thousand throng the countryside to hear Him, but He has a conversation with Andrew and a boy who has brought his lunch.

The crowds fill the road into Jericho to see Him,

[1]Mt. 9:36
[2]Jn. 10:3,13-15,28

but He seeks out a curious little man in a sycamore tree, and enters Zaccheus' house.

A dinner party is given in His honor, but of all the important contacts He could be making, He has time only to forgive the sins of a woman from the streets. Institutions miss the individual. Jesus made no such mistake.

"When He saw the multitudes, He was moved with compassion on them, because they fainted. . . ." Do crowds really look that way? Do people seem to be fainting when you see them scurrying about in a busy shopping district? Do they look helpless at a downtown intersection? Hardly. But when Jesus sees humanity, behind all that scurrying madness and feverish activity, He sees the fainting heart, the lonely life, the helplessness.

"All we like sheep have gone astray,"[3] said Isaiah, as he expressed God's viewpoint of man. The people of Isaiah's time, the people of Jesus' time, and the people of our time are not essentially different. Crowds always look carefree and content. They are busily occupied. But with the eyes of Jesus we can look behind the false front, and see loneliness, emptiness, and helplessness. Even in the strongest, the most powerful, the rebellious.

In a striking letter to a pastor in the German Democratic Republic, in which he advises Christians to remain under an atheistic regime, Karl Barth writes:

"You should accept none of your countrymen at their own estimate. Don't ever honor them as the

---
[3]Isa. 53:6

unbelieving and strong men they pretend to be!
. . . .You as Christians must confidently claim that
your atheists belong to God as much as you do.
Whether they will be converted may be more doubt-
ful. There is a sound basis. . . .for you to stand and
to bear witness to them of the Lord who died and
rose again for them, also. . . .The grace of the
gospel. . . .does not demand, it gives."[4]

Such is the compassion in Jesus' eyes for all men.
"When He *saw* the multitudes. . ."

Where did this compassion come from? Look
now, if you can, on the heart of Jesus. "When He
saw the multitudes, He was moved." Whatever compassion is reflected in His eyes comes from His
heart. He is moved to the depths of His being.

Although these words were not written about
Jesus only, they find their complete fulfillment in
Him:

"Who is so low that I am not his brother?
Who is so high that I've no path to him?

Who is so poor I may not feel his hunger?
Who is so rich I may not pity him?

Who is so hurt I may not know his heartache?
Who sings for joy my heart may never share?

Who in God's heaven has passed beyond my
        vision?
Who in hell's depths where I may never fare?"[5]

Someone has said: "If a perfect man existed in a

---

[4]Karl Barth, "How To Serve God In A Marxist Land," Association
Press, p. 57, 58

[5]S. Ralph Harlow, "Who Is So Low," quoted in Masterpieces of
Religious Verse, Edited by James Dalton Morrison, p. 465

world such as ours, he would die of horror and compassion at the terrible things that happen in it every second." A perfect Man did exist. He died of compassion.

But the love in Jesus' heart is really the revelation of the love of God for man! When we see Jesus, we see God. "Anyone who has seen Me has seen the Father."[6] The compassionate Christ reveals the compassionate God.

Therefore we hear Jesus tell the story of a son who squandered his father's money, lived it up, away from home, came back, repentant yet expecting nothing, and his father "saw him and had compassion, and ran, and fell on his neck, and kissed him."[7] God is like that father, full of compassion for his lost son(s). Therefore we hear Jesus speak of a servant who piled up such an incredible debt that he could never repay his master, and when he appealed for mercy and patience, "the lord of that servant was moved with compassion. . . .and forgave him that debt."[8] God is like that master, compassionate and forgiving. The heart of Jesus is the revelation of the heart of God.

But how is it possible that God can love us, when we squander everything He has given us, when we rebel against Him and run up an unpayable debt? How can it possibly be that Jesus in His purity and perfection can love the outcast and the sinner? Does He not see our selfishness? Does He not abhor our rebellion? Is He blind to our evil deeds and thoughts?

[6] Jn. 14:9
[7] Lk. 15:21
[8] Mt. 18:27

42

Of course Jesus knows and abhors our sins. But He loves us. . . . How can this be?

In that dramatic book about World War I, "All Quiet On The Western Front," there is a scene where a German soldier, attacking the English, leaps into a shell-hole and finds an Englishman there. At the first shock he stiffens, readies his bayonet. Suddenly he discovers that the English soldier is seriously wounded, and is touched by his condition. He takes out his canteen and gives the wounded man a drink. The Englishman gives him a look of gratitude and points to his own breast pocket. The German takes an envelope from the pocket. Some pictures of the man's family drop out. In that moment before the English soldier dies, the German holds up before him the pictures of his wife and children and mother.

Now, what has happened? The attacker who at first saw only the man as an enemy, in an enemy uniform, ready to kill or be killed, is suddenly transformed and looks upon him as a suffering human being. He sees him not as an enemy. He sees a man in pain. He sees him as a human being who loves, and who is loved by his wife and children. He has compassion on him.

There are two ways of seeing. We can see all the hatred, the bitterness, the rebellious selfishness of men, which is surely there for us to behold. Or we can see mankind as lost children, as "sheep having no shepherd." Jesus knows people are hateful and malicious. He knows it better than we. But He sees them as lost children of His Father—lost and on the wrong road. This is one of the mysteries of the New

Testament, that Jesus can say from the cross: "Father, forgive them; for they know not what they do."[9]

Jesus does not have to fight down his feelings of hatred. Jesus does not have to stifle His contempt for His enemies. The compassion in His heart is genuine; His is a different way of seeing! God's compassion is genuine, too. God looks on humanity in love. "When He saw the multitudes, He was moved with compassion on them. . . ."

Now lower your eyes and take a look at Jesus' hands, and you will see these hands full of compassion, also. These hands that touched the leper, healed the blind, raised the dead, encouraged the fallen. "And Jesus . . . saw a great multitude, and was moved with compassion toward them, and He healed their sick."[10] He saw. He was moved. He healed. His compassion leads to action.

The man was out of his mind. Jesus saw him in that pitiable condition, tormenting his own body, tormented in his mind, and He was moved with a divine pity. He touched the maniac, healed him, and said: "Go home to thy friends, and tell them how great things the Lord hath done for thee, and hath had compassion on thee."[11]

She was a widow and now she had lost her only son. Tragedy had followed tragedy and she was bowed down under the burden of her suffering. The funeral procession passed Jesus. He was touched by her suffering and felt the burden as His own. "When the Lord saw her, He had compassion on her, and

[9] Lk. 23:34
[10] Mt. 14:14
[11] Mk. 5:9

said unto her, Weep not."[12] He stopped the procession, raised the dead, and handed the boy to his mother.

He was teaching in the synagogue. And there was a woman who had been crippled for eighteen years. Eighteen long years of misery. And Jesus moved to compassion as He felt the weight of her suffering, laid His hands on her and healed her. These hands fed the multitude but gave them more than bread. These hands healed the sick, but gave them more than health. These hands touched the sinner, but gave him more than encouragement. These hands expressed the pity of God, as well as the suffering of the Son of man. He who began to identify Himself with us in baptism, identifies Himself with us in our sorrows and makes us whole.

These hands began no economic reform, initiated no political action, started no social transformation. These hands were given over to His enemies, laid on a cross, pierced by nails, torn in agony, hurt for a wearisome world. Even the resurrected Jesus bears the nailprints in His hands for all to see.

"And one shall say unto Him, 'What are these wounds in Thine hands?'

"Then He shall answer, 'Those with which I was wounded in the house of My friends.' "[13]

Look closely at the portrait and you will see the nailprints in His hands—the compassion Jesus demonstrates for our salvation. Let His hands touch you, as they touched the sick, and heal you in body, mind and spirit. Let His hands convey the love of

---

[12]Lk. 7:13
[13]Zech. 13:6

45

God to you, making you whole. Let the nailpierced hands move you to compassion, also. . . .

Now take a final look at the portrait of the compassionate Christ. The compassion in His heart is also expressed with His mouth. "Moved with compassion toward them, because they were as sheep not having a shepherd . . . He began to teach them many things."[14] He saw. He was moved. He taught. He must proclaim the love of God. He must preach good tidings. God—the unseen God, the hidden God —God is a Father full of compassion and mercy. Jesus proclaims the gospel of a compassionate God:

"Blessed are the poor in spirit: for theirs is the kingdom of heaven."

"Blessed are they that mourn: for they shall be comforted."

"Come unto Me, all ye that labor and are heavy laden, and I will give you rest."

"I will have mercy and not sacrifice: for I am not come to call the righteous, but sinners to repentance."[15]

His disciples must proclaim it after Him: "He was moved with compassion . . . Then saith He unto his disciples, the harvest truly is plenteous, but the laborers are few, Pray ye therefore the Lord of the harvest, that He will send forth laborers into His harvest."[16] The task is enormous. The time is short. The harvest is near. The witness must continue. The good tidings proclaimed!

But all the words from Jesus' mouth do not sound

---

[14]Mk. 6:34
[15]Mt. 5:3,4;9:13;11:28
[16]Mt. 9:36-38

so compassionate. "You hypocrites! Ye shut up the kingdom of heaven against men: for ye neither go in yourselves, neither suffer ye them that are entering to go in. Woe unto you, scribes and Pharisees, hypocrites! for ye make clean the outside of the cup and of the platter, but within they are full of extortion and excess. Ye serpents . . . how can ye escape the damnation of hell?"[17] These thundering judgments came from His lips, also.

Now, such words are not prompted by contempt. We know how wrong it is for us to hold humanity in contempt or even to despise one single person. When we despise another, we can never help him. How can Jesus save anyone if He despises him? Surely Jesus does not speak from motives of contempt, or else He could never have prayed for His enemies on the Cross. God does not despise man and condemn him to hell. The very opposite is true. God loves man and becomes Man for man's sake. "God sent not His Son into the world to condemn the world; but that the world through Him might be saved."[18]

Then, if Jesus is not moved by contempt when He speaks so harshly, what is His motivation? Compassion! Consider what prompts the shepherd to leave the ninety-and-nine to seek that lost sheep? Is it not the loss of that sheep, the consequences of loss and the shepherd's compassion lest that sheep be lost?

"All we like sheep have gone astray; we have turned every one to his own way."[19] And what are

17Mt. 23:13,25,33
18Jn. 3:17
19Isa. 53:6

47

the consequences? "The wages of sin is death."[20]
"There shall be weeping and gnashing of teeth."[21]
The straying sheep will be lost. Jesus knows the
consequences and therefore He tells us the truth. His
violent words about hell and damnation spring from
His compassion for all straying and shepherdless
sheep who remain forever outside the fold. He has
come to call us into His fold with truth and love.

He is always motivated by compassion. His words
are full of saving power for the fallen. Jesus never
drove anyone away. Anyone who comes in humble
repentance, expecting help, is encouraged. "Him that
cometh to Me, I will in no wise cast out."[22] This
means compassion without limits. We may set limits.
Jesus never does. He is moved with a divine pity
when you ask for mercy.

And God is like that, too. His love is limitless. He
forgives your unpayable debts. He welcomes you
back home. He has affirmed His love with the blood
of His Son. This is the good news in Jesus' mouth,
the news of a compassionate God. "When he saw the
multitudes, he was moved with compassion on
them, because they fainted, and were scattered
abroad, as sheep having no shepherd." He saw. He
was moved. He healed. He taught.

As you gaze on this portrait, you, too, will become
compassionate. James Hannington was the first
Bishop of Eastern Equatorial Africa. Witnessing for
Christ he went to one tribe after another, but fell
into the hands of savages and was slain by a native.

[20]Rom. 6:23
[21]Mt. 25:30
[22]Jn. 6:37

48

Years later the son of James Hannington heard the call of God. He felt led to the same field where his father had died, a Christian martyr. He went to that tribe. He searched for the man who had killed his father. And when the son of James Hannington found him, he proclaimed the grace of God in Jesus Christ. The native became a Christian and was baptized.

The world has killed our Lord Jesus Christ. Now we, His brethren, must go in compassion and concern, identifying ourselves with suffering humanity. Go with compassion in *our* eyes, in *our* hands, in *our* mouths, and especially in *our* hearts. Go, bringing the lost sheep into the fold and to the Shepherd. Go, with that compassion which only the compassionate Christ can give us. "Freely ye have received, freely give."[23]

---

[23]Mt. 10:8

CHAPTER 5

THE COMMENDING JESUS

"I have not found so great faith, no, not in Israel" (Mt. 8:10)

A popular psychologist advocates in his nationally syndicated column, that his readers become members of his Compliment Club. He suggests they compliment more than they do, since people like to be praised. Not a bad idea. But he wants them to hand out compliments lavishly, like someone on a street corner handing out free literature, in order that they themselves may become more successful. Commend your boss and you are on the way up the ladder!

We immediately sense something wrong. A sincere compliment, yes. But compliments passed out indiscriminately for selfish gain, no! When most motion pictures are advertised as "colossal," "the greatest," "the finest," "the best," then these words lose their meaning. When everything is "fabulous," nothing is "fabulous" any longer.

The Greeks had a proverb for it: "Many men know how to flatter; few to praise." Apple-polishers abound, but those who know how to commend sincerely are few.

In the New Testament I am impressed by the compliments of Jesus, compliments sparingly given. In no sense is He trying to flatter in order to be successful, or get on the good side of people. His commendations are rare. Yet this very scarcity enhances their value like precious stones. Let us look at the painting of the commending Christ. The people whom He commends will appear in it, also. But for what does He praise them? What is praiseworthy and commendable in them?

As Jesus entered Capernaum, a city on the Sea of Galilee and a Roman military post, a Roman centurion, a commander of one hundred men, approached Him:

"Sir, a boy of mine lies at home paralyzed and racked with pain."

Jesus said: "I will come and cure him."

The centurion replied: "Sir, who am I to have you under my roof? You need only say the word and the boy will be cured. I know, for I am myself under orders, with soldiers under me. I say to one, 'Go,' and he goes; to another, 'Come here,' and he comes; and to my servant, 'Do this,' and he does it."

He believed only a word from Jesus would bring healing. Jesus heard him with astonishment. Then He said:

"I tell you this: nowhere, even in Israel, have I found such faith."[1] He told the centurion to go home; and he would discover the boy cured.

Never does Jesus give such a compliment on faith, though often He speaks of its importance. Almost every account of healing involves faith: "According

[1]Mt. 8:6-10

53

to your faith be it unto you." But this Roman is told that his faith outshines all the others, even of Israel. Why?

His army training had made him conscious of authority. He gives orders and his men obey. He commands and they carry out that command. He is under orders, too. When his superior officer issues an order, he must carry it out. The centurion now simply transfers such authority to the realm of the spirit.

"Jesus is under authority, the authority of God," the centurion is really saying, "when He commands, He commands with authority. He has the power of God. Evil powers obey, illness is cured, and His authority goes unquestioned." Jesus commends him for this insight into the spiritual world. He commends him because he has recognized Jesus as a man of God with and under authority.

How simple faith really is! Do you find it hard to believe? Faith is not foreign to you. Faith is native to you. Faith is not something you have to work up or pump in from the outside. You have faith already. You practice faith daily.

You step on a bus, pay your fare, take a seat and relax while you trust the bus driver to take you through perilous traffic. You put your faith in him. You get your paycheck, put it in the bank, and trust the banker that your money is safe, even though you may have read recently about an embezzler. You feel sick, go to the doctor, trust him to find out what is wrong with you, expect him to help you, and unreservedly commit yourself to his authority.

You already have faith. This is not *religious* faith.

Jesus commends a Roman, not a Jew, a man who was not of the "religious community." Again and again the gospel is proclaimed to men who have faith already, and who transfer this every-day faith into the spiritual realm. Such faith Jesus commends, which recognizes Him as having the power of God, and which honors His authority over suffering and sin.

"Nowhere, even in Israel,
have I found such faith."

Of the twelve whom Jesus chose to be His disciples, only one is commended at the beginning of his discipleship. Most of the twelve were called by a direct command to follow. This one received a compliment which, in turn, changed the direction of his whole life. Without that compliment it would be safe to say, Nathanael may never have become a disciple of Jesus. Jesus knows when to commend and when to keep silent.

Nathanael was a prejudiced man. His friend, Philip, came to him with the news that he had found the Messiah of Israel, and that He was a Man from Nazareth named Jesus.

"Can there any good thing come out of Nazareth?" Nathanael asked.

They were good friends and Philip was not shocked. In his practical manner he only answered: "Come and see." Nathanael did come. When Jesus saw them both coming, He said to Nathanael: "Behold an Israelite indeed, in whom is no guile."[2]

That compliment was the turning point. Nathanael

---

[2]Jn. 1:45-47

started talking to the Man who came from this uneventful, low-class burg—Nazareth. Their conversation caused him to follow Jesus.

"No guile." No deceitfulness or craftiness was in this son of Jacob. Not that Nathanael was without fault. He had already betrayed his prejudices, which Jesus did not excuse, but which He will deal with later. Nor was Nathanael born without deceit. Rather, Nathanael was a disciplined man. He consciously practiced living without deceit. For this discipline Jesus commends him.

Nathanael disciplined himself before he became a Christian. The Roman centurion had faith before coming to Jesus and transferred that faith to the spiritual realm. Nathanael practiced discipline before becoming an apostle, and this discipline is only the beginning of all Jesus will demand from him: "If any man will come after Me, let him deny himself, and take up his cross, and follow Me."[3]

"The Imitation of Christ" asks the question: "Who hath a harder struggle than he that laboureth to conquer himself?" Knowing the hardness of the struggle, we are likely to give up before we start. We think it is impossible to control ourselves, but we must not think of possibility and impossibility. Rather, we ought to attempt control.

When faced with a compulsory question on an examination, better attempt to do the best you can. You may get somewhere. You surely will get nowhere if you don't make an attempt. The same goes for climbing a mountain or learning how to swim,

[3]Mt. 16:24

56

even for prying loose a zipper that got stuck half-way up. For those attempts, for this trying and discipline, Jesus commends Nathanael. And such discipline will become stronger with use, as God gives help to overcome.

> "Behold an Israelite indeed,
> in whom is no guile."

It will be two years before we hear Jesus commend any of His disciples so laudably again. Two years; praise scarce as gold is of great worth. They had gone to Caesarea Philippi, a city once associated with the worship of Baal, where the Greeks claimed their god of nature, Pan, was born, and which now displayed a white marble temple for the worship of Caesar. Here comes a homeless wandering preacher from Galilee with his little company of uneducated village-bred bumpkins. Surrounded by the memories of the old Canaanite and Greek gods, in the presence of the symbol of Roman power and divinity, Jesus asks a leading question:

"Who do you say that I am?"

Peter is quick to reply: "You? You are Christ, the Son of the Living God!"[4]

"I know it is no light matter," Peter seems to be saying, "I know it is no light matter to call anyone the Son of God. Surely, here amid all these memories of idolatry and in the midst of this blasphemous assertion that Caesar is divine, I must beware. But even here I do not shrink from the assertion that you are the long-awaited Messiah. Even here, in my strict monotheistic belief in one God, I say there is

---

[4]Mt. 16:15,16 Phillips

no other explanation for what I have seen and heard these years in your presence, but that you are the Son of the Living God."

And Jesus said: "Simon, son of Jonah, you are a fortunate man, indeed! For it was not your own nature, but my Heavenly Father Who has revealed this truth to you!"[5]

Jesus thanks His heavenly Father for this revelation, for truth must always be revealed. We can only discover truth in the sense that we respond to God's revelation. Therefore Jesus commends His disciple for this openness to truth. It may have taken Peter two years to arrive at this stage, but then the moment has come and Jesus' patience is rewarded.

In a certain sense this openness to revelation was Peter's before he became a Christian. He responded to Jesus' call to follow Him. Not many would leave their business and go wandering around the countryside without a steady income. Peter had. He was open to the call, and now he is open to God's revelation in Christ.

What if Peter had not been receptive to the truth? What if no one had been willing to acknowledge Jesus as the Son of God? For two years the trouble had not lain with the transmission of the Word of God, but with the reception of the instruments. For two years Jesus had not forced His identity on the apostles. He was not about to change His methods. They must respond. They must be open to God. They must find God in Jesus.

When they do—when we do—meaning is found

---

[5]Mt. 16:17 Phillips

to the drama of the New Testament. Unless they do—unless we do—that New Testament remains a mere collection of interesting stories and sayings. But when we acknowledge God in Christ, when we know God sent His only Son into the world, then we find the key which unlocks all mysteries, to God and Jesus, to life and eternity. Revelation is vital, but Jesus commends response to God's truth, and openness to that revelation.

"Simon, son of Jonah,
   You are a fortunate man, indeed,
   For it was not your own nature
   But my Heavenly Father
   Who has revealed this truth to you."

We cannot assimilate into this portrait all the commendations of the commending Christ. But, surely, one other extraordinary compliment stands out. Two days before His death Jesus has supper in Bethany at the house of a man identified as Simon, the leper. The meal takes place in an open courtyard, a very public occasion. A woman comes with a box of perfumed ointment, which is of such great value that it is meant to be used only a few drops at a time. She pours the entire contents over Jesus' head. The disciples who have endured privation in His company, consider this a fantastic waste.

"Couldn't this perfume have been sold for a lot of money and the proceeds given to the poor?" they ask.

Jesus answers: "Why must you make this woman feel uncomfortable? She has done a beautiful thing for me. You have the poor with you always, but you will not always have me. When she poured this perfume on my body, she was preparing it for my burial." Jesus commends this woman for her act of love and has such confidence in His life-work, that He adds: "I tell you plainly that wherever the gospel is preached in the whole world, this act of hers will also be told in memory of her."[6]

He knows He is to die. He cannot forget His destiny—the Cross. Did that woman know for what she had anointed Him? She may have thought only of His Triumphant entry into Jerusalem a few days ago. Now, in an impulsive act, she anoints Him as Israel's Messiah-King. If that is her motive, Jesus' commendation is the more touching. There will be a crown—of thorns. There will be a coronation—upon a cross.

"She has done a beautiful thing for Me." Love always has some extravagance in it. Love never stops to calculate. Love is not afraid of people. Love does not say, "What will everyone think of this?" Love acts, knowing full well there are certain moments in life which come, never to return again. Jesus commends her for her love.

As the Roman centurion is commended for faith which he already had; as Nathanael is commended for discipline which was his prior to his apostleship; as Peter is commended for his openness to God's revelation, an openness he has shown from the beginning; so this woman is commended for love which brings her to Jesus' feet. This love when laid at His feet now experiences the acceptance of God and the smile of Jesus.

---

[6]Mt. 26:9-13

But, since God made us, *He* has given us the capacity to believe, the strength for discipline, the openness to revelation, the extravagance of love. All are His gifts. Now, in the presence of the commending Christ we see that all comes from God. This is the importance of the portrait of the commending Christ.

He takes what little we bring and transforms it for His Kingdom. He commends a Roman for his faith, and that centurion suddenly realizes faith can move mountains in the spiritual realm. He commends the discipline of Nathanael, and Nathanael slowly awakens to the truth that his discipleship has been only the beginning compared with the rigors Jesus will demand. He commends the response of Peter, and Peter will see that if only he is receptive to more revelation, he will open doors for Jews and Gentiles and in Rome itself. He commends the love of that woman, and she will see *His* love for all mankind, as He sacrifices Himself. Dimly she will learn that we are to love as He loved us!

All this the commending Christ does when the little we bring to Him is ignited by His pertinent, well-timed compliments, and our tiny sparks burst forth into mighty flames. Even for us the commending Christ has compliments in Scripture.

For our faith: "Thomas, because you have seen Me, you have found faith. Happy are they who never saw Me and yet have found faith."[7]

For disciplined lives: "EVERYONE who hath forsaken houses, or brethren, or sisters, or father, or

---

[7] Jn. 20:29 English

mother, or wife, or children, or lands, for My name's sake, shall receive an hundredfold, and shall inherit everlasting life."[8]

For love: "Whosoever shall give to drink unto one of these little ones a cup of cold water only . . . shall in no wise lose his reward."[9]

Let us strive for those qualities which Jesus commends, and lay all His gifts to us at His feet, that in heaven we may hear the greatest commendation of all: For, there in heaven, it will not matter so much what we receive, whether harps or crowns or white robes, but only if we may hear the commending Christ say:

"Well done, good and faithful servant;
enter into the joy of your Master."[10]

[8]Mt. 19:29
[9]Mt. 10:42
[10]Mt. 25:21 RSV

CHAPTER 6

THE CALLING JESUS

*"Come unto me, all ye
that labor and are heavy laden,
and I will give you rest" (Mt. 11:28)*

The most primitive idea about God is God in
competition with men. The gods are above; men
below. If men raise themselves and become prosperous or great, the gods begrudge it. They are jealous.
They do not like competition. Some of us still retain
such primitive notions about God. We explore space.
God does not like it, we think. We are afraid that the
bigger we get, the more powerful we grow in knowledge and achievement, the more jealous God will be.

As men developed in their thought God became
more and more the great Unknown. He was—whatever He was—detached from the world, the Unknowable. Plato thought it was difficult to find out
anything about God, and whatever could be found
out could not possibly be told to anyone else. For
Lucretius the gods exist in their remote majesty. And
according to the Stoics God is utterly detached from
the human scene, and we cannot influence Him.
Many still retain these ideas. God is Unknowable; in

the beyond. He does not care. He is completely removed from the world. He is quite indifferent.

Even to the Jews God is the Holy One, the Unapproachable One. A curtain hangs in the temple to hide Him. Only once a year the high priest may enter to make atonement for the people. He alone can come near the holy, set apart One, the God Who is separated from man.

"Who shall ascend into the hill of the Lord?
Or who shall stand in his holy place?
He that hath clean hands, and a pure heart;
Who hath not lifted up his soul unto vanity,
    not sworn deceitfully.
He shall receive the blessing from the Lord,
And righteousness from the God of his
    salvation."[1]

Who can approach the hill of the Lord? Who can achieve and ascend and *stand* in his holy place with clean hands and a pure heart? The door slams in our face when we hear this! How can anyone get near to this "Holy Other?"

And Jesus comes into this world where God is high and holy, remote and removed, unapproachable and unknowable, and reverses our main conception of God. Jesus comes to call us to God. Jesus comes with the news that God is not in competition with men, that God is not removed from us, that He wants us to approach Him, that, in fact, this holy God is friendly to sinners. For this reason the scribes and Pharisees were filled with horror when they saw Jesus befriending the common people. But Jesus re-

---
[1]Ps. 24:3-5

veals God, enters the human scene, and calls us to Him:

"Come unto Me, all ye that labor and are heavy laden, and I will give you rest. Take my yoke upon you, and learn of Me . . ."[2] Surely, this is one of the most beautiful of all the portraits in this gallery, in which Jesus reverses our human ideas of God and says: "God actually wants you to come to Him. God calls you as a father calls his children home. God seeks you as a shepherd seeks a lost sheep. I call you in His Name. Learn of Me . . . ye shall find rest unto your souls. For my yoke is easy, and my burden is light."[3]

Jesus calls us to salvation: "Come unto me, all ye that labor." Many voices call but what do they offer?

Shakespeare calls and says: "Come unto me, and I will give you literature."

Browning calls and says: "Come unto me, and I will give you poetry."

Kant calls and says: "Come unto me, and I will give you philosophy."

Sartre calls and says: "Come unto me, and I will give you existentialism."

Freud calls and says: "Come unto me, and I will give you psychoanalysis."

Einstein calls and says: "Come unto me, and I will give you science."

The medical profession calls and says: "Come unto me, and I will give you health."

The newspaper calls and says: "Come unto me, and I will give you information."

[2]Mt. 11:28
[3]Mt. 11:29-30

The motion picture industry calls and says: "Come unto me, and I will give you entertainment."

The advertisers call and say: "Come unto me, and I will give you better living."

Everything the world offers is temporal. Everything Jesus offers is eternal! He calls us to salvation, but He calls a special group.

Overcome by the hardness and callousness of intellectuals, the so-called wise of the world, and after observing their incredulity and refusal to believe, Jesus prayed: "I thank Thee, Father, Lord of heaven and earth, for hiding these things from the learned and wise, and revealing them to the simple. Yes, Father, such was Thy choice . . ."[4] Now He turns to these "simple": "Come unto me, all ye that labor and are heavy laden." The person whom Jesus calls is a burdened person, a person humble enough to acknowledge his weight.

"Sin and the sense of sin will always be with us," writes Julian Huxley, "But . . . the religion of the future will try to prevent men's being afflicted with the sense of sin, rather than encourage it and then attempt to cure it."[5] But, how can we prevent this sense of sin? Not that Jesus ever encourages it—never. He does not impose the burden. He does not preach to produce guilt. He knows the burden is there already, and He offers a cure.

In fact, many people suffer from the illusion that they are unique. No one else has their difficulties. No one else can have the doubts they have. No one else can be quite as wicked or nearly so weak. Jesus

---

[4]Mt. 11:25,26
[5]J. Huxley, "Religion Without Revelation," Harper, p. 160

knows this. He calls precisely those who feel in a class by themselves, lumps all human problems together, and says: "Come unto me, *all* ye that labor and are heavy laden, and I will give you rest."

What is Jesus' cure? "Come unto ME." A call not to join an organization, to follow an ethic, a new teaching, or even a way of life, but a call to meet a Person—an invitation to come directly to Him, and through Him to God. He is the Door. He is the Way.

God desires to be approached. God can be approached through Jesus. Can anyone hold an intimate conversation with one of the Greek gods or with the Holy Other of the Old Testament? But the Father of Jesus Christ offers Himself to us: "Come unto Me."

And if we come—"salvation." That is, the burden lifted, the weight removed. "I will give you rest." The release of sin. The removal of every fear. Freedom of conscience. Everlasting Life. "Salvation comes only as the result of a vision of God," says D. T. Niles. Jesus brings us the vision of God—the God Who desires to be approached. "It is not the fear of sin but the love of God which sets men free."[6]

"Tell me your name," I challenged Christ.

"Were you prophet, saint supreme?

"Did you wear true flesh and blood?

"Are you that which we call God?
or but a hope, a sigh,
a thing compacted of man's dream?"

---

[6]D. T. Niles, "Seeing The Invisible," Harper, p. 147

"I will declare Myself," said Christ
"When you confess your name and station."
  Easy terms. I thought and thought
  But still the sum of me was nought.
"A dying sinner, I"
And straight He told His Name, "Salvation."
(Anna Bunston de Bary)[7]

Even more beautiful is Jesus' call to serenity. "I will give you rest." Salvation leads to serenity and peace of mind. Serenity, like salvation, is a gift. We never will obtain it through mental gymnastics or psychological pursuits, by repeating prayers or reciting verses, but only through an encounter with Jesus. Bring your burden to Him. Let Him have it. Accept His offer. Let His peace fill you.

Serenity becomes yours through utter faith in God; not by pretending to believe or half believing, but by believing in the God revealed through Jesus, Who numbers the hairs on our heads, and knows when every sparrow falls; Who is the Creator of the universe, but actually wants to be our Father; Who enters this world to identify Himself with us and in Jesus extends His grace, compassion, and love: "I will give you REST." Accept this offer.

Many other voices call us to peace, but the approach is quite different from Jesus' invitation. These other voices invite us on a trip to a South Sea Isle where the palm trees sway and a luscious beach calls us to play, where at eventide there is the ultimate in entertainment. The travel posters of the world invite us to swim and ski, dine and dance, relax

[7]"Masterpieces of Religious Verse," James Dalton Morrison, Editor, p. 215

and enjoy, and who can deny there *is* relaxation in getting away?

But what is the thought behind this approach? Produce a perfect set of circumstances and you will have peace! Peace comes when you can get away from everyday pressures. Peace comes when the waters are still, the wind dies down, and the surface is calm. Yet what goes on beneath the surface? Why do many who seem to achieve perfect circumstances with money and leisure still frequent the psychiatrist?

Jesus does not offer a perfect set of circumstances or still waters on life's surface, but peace in our hearts—calm beneath the surface. His rest is not escapism. The waters may be quite turbulent and the winds may blow. Serenity is not immunity from trouble. Christians, after all, have their share of suffering. They do not go through life unharmed. They have been thrown to the lions and burned at the stake. They may be killed in war or lose their only child. Serenity of the soul is quietness beneath these troubled waters. Not a perfect set of circumstances, but peace in the midst of the most trying circumstances: "Peace I leave with you, my peace I give unto you. . . . Let not your heart be troubled, neither let it be afraid."[8]

How? How can a man find peace when he is out of work? Or a mother of four left alone trying to make ends meet? Or when nerves are stretched to the breaking point and nothing seems to go right? Jesus offers *His* peace. Not ours, *His*. "I will give

---

[8]Jn. 14:27

70

you rest."

Look at Him—did anyone ever see Him irritated, nervous, upset? And yet He endured intrusions into His privacy, the demands of inconsiderate people, misunderstandings, criticisms, pettiness, disappointments, the burdens of sharing people's hurts and feeling their sorrows and sins as His own. But no sign of strain, no trace of nerves.

Such peace is within your reach. Whatever life may do to you, Jesus can hold you steady and serene. His peace is potentially yours. He offers it. You may have it. It is a gift. If only you will believe Him.

> "I heard the voice of Jesus say,
> 'Come unto me and rest;
> Lay down, thou weary one,
> Lay down thy head upon my breast.'

> "I came to Jesus as I was,
> Weary and worn and sad,
> I found in him a resting place,
> And He has made me glad."

"I will give you rest."

The beauty of the calling Christ is not only in His call to salvation and His call to serenity, but also in His call to service. "Take my yoke upon you." The yoke is to feel useful in service. We want to do something. Often in the Church ministers are over-concerned, looking for more jobs for people to do. When Jesus calls a man to Him, He gives him a job. "Take my yoke."

A yoke has two loops or bows. A yoke brings two

oxen together to do one job. As both pull the load, the yoke actually lightens the workload. The yoke of Christ binds me to my fellowman to do the work of the kingdom together. He sets us to work for God. And what is more noble service to humanity than binding up the sorely wounded, healing broken hearts, visiting the sick, the imprisoned, the needy, and witnessing in love to the good news of Jesus Christ?

"TAKE my yoke . . . my yoke is easy." The rabbis spoke of the yoke of law. Peter's question to the Jerusalem council, as the council discussed the enforcement of Jewish law to Gentile converts, reflects that view: "Why tempt ye God to put a yoke upon the neck of the disciples, which neither our fathers nor we were able to bear?"[9]

That is not Jesus' yoke. His yoke is not a burden, for He calls the burdened to rest. His yoke is not heavy laden, for He says it is 'easy.' His yoke is not inflicted law for it is 'light.' Easy? Light? Was His yoke easy when they were plotting His death? Was His yoke easy when many who had followed Him walked no longer with Him? Was His yoke easy when one of His friends betrayed Him? Was His yoke easy when the world which He had come to save crucified Him, and He hung there, bloody and beaten? How can it be easy?

He serves God. He knows His Father. He is at peace. He is calm beneath the surface. He knows why He is alive. He knows why He has come to earth. He knows where He is going. He knows God.

[9]Acts 15:10

God is with Him. This makes the yoke 'easy.' This makes the service 'light.' No burden of a guilty conscience. No negative commands to pinch the soul. No restrictives binding and imprisoning Him, creating fear. He is free. He sets us free.

He invites us to share the secret of His yoke: "Learn of Me." He is "meek and lowly in heart." He knows man's insignificance on the face of the earth, and yet his significance to the Almighty God. He is humble—"learn." From somewhere He taps secret springs of living water. From somewhere He receives strength in weakness.

We shall find His freedom as we learn of Him, take His yoke upon us, and serve mankind the way He did! Jesus is with us not simply because we accepted His call to salvation or receive His serenity, but Jesus is with us in a unique sense when we enter His service, and get under His yoke. In service we receive more inner peace, for Jesus repeats this promise of rest *after* we have taken His yoke.

Or to put it another way: Jesus is with us not only when we need Him, but also because He needs us. He is with us not only because He is our Saviour, but also when He becomes our Lord. "Take my yoke, *and* ye shall find rest unto your souls." More rest, more calm, more joy promised in service.

So Jesus calls you. He invites you to the eternal God who wants to be approached. For this God approaches you in Jesus and invites you to salvation, serenity, and service. You may come from the lowest of motives. You may only want peace of mind, or rest for your burdens. Whatever the motive, come!

For your experience will be the same as that Christian who said: "I came looking for shelter. I found a shell. And then in that shell, I found a pearl."

"Come until Me, all ye that labor and
are heavy laden, and I will give you rest."

CHAPTER 7

THE POWERFUL JESUS

"If I cast out devils by the Spirit of God, then the kingdom of God is come unto you"
(Mt. 12:28)

When we think of power we think of machines and muscle, magnificent displays of scientific achievement, man's ability to change the elements. Nation lifts up sword against nation and the mightiest conquers in the strife; the one with the most weapons is the most powerful. Or, an athlete who runs, jumps, swims, boxes, lifts, achieves, breaks records is our hero. Our symbol of power? Atlas, the mighty Atlas, who carries the world on his back. This kind of power we may also observe in Jesus.

There is another kind of power—the power of love. The symbol? Atlas carrying the world not externally, but internally, not on his back, but in his heart! This is the power of the new covenant which prophets announce and disciples pen, the power not of outer law but inner force, not written on stone, but written in the heart. This is the energy that overcomes temptation, breaks an evil habit. The prisoner is set free by the saving might of Christ. This is the portrait of the powerful Christ—bold and brave—the brush-strokes vivid, the colors stirring, the impact dynamic.

If we look for external might we shall find it in Jesus' power over nature. He controls the forces of nature. There comes to mind that fascinating tale of the turbulent storm on the Sea of Galilee. The wind whips up the waves perhaps six feet high, the ship tosses to and fro, the water spills into the boat, the seasoned, experienced fishermen bail out, filled with fear, and the poised figure of Jesus rebukes the wind! "He . . . said unto the sea, Peace, be still. And the wind ceased, and there was a great calm."[1]

We may question the miracle, but one look at the story itself is sufficient proof. Once you *see* the ship riding the waves, and the fear riding on the fishermen's faces; once you *feel* the water splashing and sense the miraculous calm settle on nature; once you *hear* the disciples mutter to each other: "What manner of man is this, that even the wind and the sea obey him,"[2] then you cannot escape the power of Christ.

And . . . . the fig tree. Jesus comes looking for fruit, but finds none. The tree is in leaf, promising fruit, but no fruit. Jesus says: "Let no fruit grow on thee henceforward forever." This fig tree is a symbol of Israel—and can become a symbol of a barren church—with promises of spiritual products, but mere promises. The next day the disciples are dumbfounded. "How soon is the fig tree withered away!"[3]

[1]Mk. 4:39
[2]Mk. 4:41
[3]Mt. 21:19,20

"All power is given unto me in heaven and in earth," says Jesus.[4] And if we do not dispute that statement, why should we dispute the lesser miracles involving trees, wind and sea? One thing is clear: the Creator has power over His creation. He commands; nature must obey.

What other explanation is there for that amazing remark which Jesus makes on His way to Jerusalem when crowds acclaim Him as their King and the religious leaders urge Him to quiet the people? He says: "I tell you that, if these should hold their peace, the stones would immediately cry out."[5] The forces of nature are at His command. He has power over all.

It follows quite naturally that Jesus has power also over disease. If He commands nature, He can command the baffling abnormalities of nature, sickness and disease. "Great multitudes came unto him, having with them those that were lame, blind, dumb, maimed, and many others, and cast them down at Jesus' feet; and He healed them."[6]

Jesus claimed miracles as His credentials. "If I do not the works of my Father, believe me not. But if I do, though ye believe not me, believe the works."[7]

These miracles are called "works of power." Divine power came forth from Jesus to heal. They are called "works of wonder" arousing amazement. Miracles as "wonder" are coupled with miracles as "signs." Signs and wonders shown by Jesus are sign-

[4]Mt. 28:18
[5]Lk. 19:40
[6]Mt. 15:30
[7]Jn. 10:37,38

posts pointing beyond themselves to the one working the miracles. The power comes from God and the wonder is in Christ.

"I should not be a Christian but for the miracles," Pascal quotes Augustine as saying, and then goes on to say for himself: "There would be no sin in disbelieving Jesus Christ if it were not for the miracles."[8]

Even His enemies admitted the power of Jesus: "What action are we taking? This man is performing many signs."[9]

They attempted to discredit His miracles. "It is only by Beelzebub, prince of devils, that this man drives the devils out." The argument was ludicrous.

"Every kingdom divided against itself goes to ruin," Jesus countered, "and no town, no household, that is divided against itself can stand. And if it is Satan who casts out Satan, Satan is divided against himself; how then can his kingdom stand? And if it is by Beelzebub that I cast out devils, by whom do your own people drive them out? If this is your argument, they themselves will refute you."

Something else is happening. Something you are too blind to see. Something marvelous and wonderful: "If it is by the Spirit of God that I drive out the devils, then be sure the kingdom of God has already come upon you. Or again, how can anyone break into a strong man's house and make off with his goods unless he has first tied the strong man up before ransacking his house?"[10]

[8]Pascal, "Pensees" Section XIII
[9]Jn. 11:47 English
[10]Mt. 12:25-29 English

The forces of evil can only be overcome by a successful burglar *outside of* the kingdom of evil. Jesus has come not to debate the existence of a devil, but to enter his domain, overpower and defeat him, and set his victims free. "The Kingdom of God is come unto you."

It will even follow that since all power is His in heaven and on earth, that He has power over the most baffling deviation of nature—over death! Three stories of such power over death are woven into the very fabric of the gospels. He raises the daughter of Jairus. He raises the son of the widow of Nain. He raises the brother of Mary and Martha, Lazarus. Not simply three people, but three persons who belong to other persons, who are seen as loved persons. And that something did happen is attested by this historical note:

"The large crowd of Jews discovered that He was there and came to the scene—not only because of Jesus but to catch sight of Lazarus, the man whom He had raised from the dead. Then the Chief Priests planned to kill Lazarus as well, because he was the reason for many of the Jews' going off and putting their faith in Jesus."[11]

But what of Jesus? Must He not have this power for Himself? For He has not come merely to advance a new teaching. He claims power over evil forces. He says He comes with an authority to bring the kingdom of God. If He cannot defeat death, then all His claims to divinity are for nought. If wicked men can overwhelm Him by death, what is all this "power in

---

[11]Jn. 12:9-11 Phillips

heaven and earth" but words? But the moment you see a truth, even a shred of truth in Him, you know death cannot stop this powerful Christ. "Destroy this temple, and in three days I will raise it up."[12]

Nobody really believed Him, of course. The men were sullen, moody and depressed that first Easter morn. The women went to anoint the body for entombment. When they saw the empty tomb, they were shocked and frightened to tears. Only when the risen Christ appeared, fear turned to faith and the wonder of it all overwhelmed them.

Jesus has made a breach in the impregnable wall of death! He has conquered. He *is* Lord. He is all-powerful. And that means this risen Christ is not a museum piece to be admired. No, by a single stroke this victorious Christ confronts the whole world again. He is the living Lord, alive forevermore. And that means I, too, can be linked to Him at any moment.

This brings us to the greatest power of all, the power of compassion, the power of love. Not power over disease or even death, not power over nature, but power over human nature. "All power is given unto me in heaven and in earth." The risen Jesus can change people. He still changes people, for He is alive. He, who carries the world in His heart, changes people by the power of His love.

This is essentially Jesus' work during His earthly ministry. He makes men whole.

He takes a brash, boisterous braggart named Peter who is spiritually as shifty as sand, and fashions him

[12]Jn. 2:19

into a solid rock, so that thousands will hear the gospel through him.

He takes a John of boiling temperament and fiery disposition and channels that fire into love and gives gentleness in place of harshness.

He takes a sinful woman twisted in all her thoughts, torn apart in her conscience, tormented by seven demons, and releases Mary of Magdala from her captivity, even gives her the honor of being the first to see Him risen from the dead.

He takes a greedy, selfish, despicable tax collector and transforms Zaccheus into a person of Christian charity and benevolence who in turn makes a deep committal: "Behold, Lord, the half of my goods I give to the poor; and if I have taken any thing from any man by false accusation, I restore him fourfold."[13]

He transforms men by the power of His love. A group of very ordinary people are forgiven for their sins, changed in their goals, given a vision, empowered with His Holy Spirit, and these Christians turn the world upside down, or shall we say, right-side up?

He enters Europe, takes hold of those dreaded uncivilized Huns, and brings forth a new people, civilized Christian nations, a Luther and a Melanchthon. In Britain the brutal sacrifices of the Druids are changed into the sacrifices of a broken heart, and Jesus produces the holiness of a Wesley as well as the hymns of a Watts. He advances into Africa, converts savages and head hunters, and through

---

[13]Lk. 19:8

dedicated missionaries they are head hunters no longer, but Christians through and through.

Can anyone ever measure the impact of Jesus on civilization? "All the armies that ever marched, and the navies that ever were built, and all the parliaments that ever sat . . . have not affected the life of man upon this earth as powerfully as that one solitary life . . ." At the peace conference in Versailles in 1919, after Woodrow Wilson had presented his plans, Clemenceau, prime minister of France, said, "He talked like Jesus Christ." Whether in sarcasm or admiration, no matter; immeasurable has been the influence of Jesus on the West (and the world).

His influence continues. A certain church recently received new members. In the group were a man who had been under sentence for non-support, a woman who had broken her parole, two former convicts, a woman who had been known as the neighborhood trouble-maker, a drug addict, and a married couple who had been jailed for drunken driving. He changed them. He is the living Lord, and that means at any moment you can be linked to Him!

There is, after all, little use in a Jesus who did things two thousand years ago but who does nothing now; who stilled the waves of the sea of Galilee but stills no storms in my heart now; who raised the dead, but raises none of us to new life now; who changed disciples, but cannot change drunks, deviates or the desperate now!

But how? How can we come in touch with this living Lord and receive His power for transformed lives? For one thing we can remember that *He* initiates the contact. He chose Peter and John, confronted Zaccheus and Mary, moved into the world through missionaries. He will encounter us. That is the revelation and the power of His love. He comes seeking us. We are lost, not He.

But we must make a move, too. Observe what Jesus has done for someone else, the freedom brought by the onrush of His power. This may lead us to a serious, adult examination of His life and words. Search with an open mind. Let prayer become a force. Ask for help. Look and learn of Him. Soon enough Jesus will step out of the pages and become a contemporary person, for He is our contemporary.

Some find Him as a result of crisis. Some, not all. Utterly defeated and downcast, they turn to God as a last resort. Even then He will not reject anyone! Pulled down by something they cannot control, (is it like the seven demons of Mary Magdalene?) they find a power greater than themselves (cannot Christ cast out these demons?). He removes a habit, releases a conscience, sets one free, changes human nature.

That is the fact—and that fact matters above all —the power of His love. Jesus is the strong Son of God, who has entered the devil's domain, overpowered the owner, plundered his house, spoiled his wares, and triumphed over every form of evil including death itself. He brings the kingdom of God: "If I cast out devils by the Spirit of God, then the kingdom of God is come unto you." This is the fact. The kingdom comes—even to you!

CHAPTER 8

THE QUESTIONING JESUS

"What is a man profited, if he shall gain the whole world and lose his own soul? Or what shall a man give in exchange for his soul?"
(Mt. 16:26)

"O my soul," says T. S. Eliot, "be prepared for him who knows how to ask questions." Questions can be embarrassing; "Did you brush your teeth today?"... probing: "What were you doing there last night?"... penetrating: "What are you living for?" ... jolting in nature, "What is a man profited, if he shall gain the whole world, and lose his own soul?" Strange, that in all the wealth of material about Jesus, in all the books ever written about Him, in all the sermons ever preached, so little is said about the questioning Christ. "O my soul, be prepared for him who knows how to ask questions."

Someone has gone to the arduous task of adding up these questions, and has found two hundred thirteen of them asked by Jesus in the gospels. (Some duplication, of course.) Therefore we must see a portrait of the questioning Christ. You have seen certain pictures that require a second and third look. This painting will keep us returning, for as we look, Christ questions us.

The questions of Jesus are sharp as an arrow, aimed with precision. They strike their mark. And their overall purpose is for decision! As that question which proved to be the turning point in His whole ministry: "Who do you say that I am?" And Peter answered: "You? You are the Christ, the Son of the Living God."[1]

"What is your opinion of Christ?"[2] A great teacher? A poetic idealist? An inspiring leader? Or the Son of the Living God? Jesus aims for decision, but the manner in which He achieves this can be categorized. And that we are going to do now, for we came to examine each one of the two hundred thirteen questions.

First, we see Jesus cutting through the jungle of muddled thinking. He aims at our minds! Our minds must be changed, for only he who is convinced will commit himself. We must be persuaded before we decide. So Jesus marshals the facts, states His case, asks His questions, and aims for our intellect.

For example, the religious leaders were looking for occasions to belittle Him. If they could show Him breaking the law of Moses, they would be able to discredit Him before the people. On a Sabbath, when no one was supposed to lift a finger (in honor of God), the disciples were hungry. They passed through a grainfield, took the grain into their hands, rubbed it, and ate it. But this rubbing the kernel free was work—and strictly forbidden for the Sabbath. The legalistic Pharisees were quick to seize the opportunity:

[1]Mt. 16:15,16 Phillips
[2]Mt. 22:42 Phillips

"Look, your disciples are doing something which is forbidden on the Sabbath."

Jesus answered: "Have you not read what David did when he and his men were hungry? He went into the House of God and ate the consecrated loaves, though neither he nor his men had a right to eat them, but only the priests. Or have you not read in the Law that on the Sabbath the priests in the temple break the Sabbath and it is not held against them? I tell you, there is something greater than the temple here."[3]

David was not a priest. He was not allowed into the holy place, and that bread was for priests only. But was not his action of necessity? Should a law of men keep men from food? What are laws for? What is considered a breach of the law? And what is the Sabbath for? Has it not been given for men, or would you suppose men have been created for the Sabbath? Jesus marshals the facts and aims at the mind.

On another occasion they 'needled him' with questions. "Obviously, you don't care for human approval. Now tell us—is it right to pay taxes to Caesar or not?"

Another group asked about a woman who had seven husbands: "Now in this 'resurrection', whose wife will she be of these seven men—for she belonged to all of them?"

A clever lawyer asked: "Master, what are we to consider the Law's greatest commandments?" Jesus

[3]Mt. 12:2-6 English

88

answered these questions. Then He asked one of His own.

"What is your opinion of Christ? Whose son is he?"

The question was easy. "The Son of David," they answered. Jesus expected it, and He asked another:

"How then does David when inspired by the Spirit call him Lord? He says—'The Lord said unto my Lord, Sit thou on my right hand, Till I put thine enemies underneath thy feet.' If David then calls him Lord, how can he be his son?"

No one was able to answer this. "From that day on no one dared ask him any further questions."[4] If only we will think about it . . . Jesus aims at our intellect that we may make up our mind in favor of truth and of the God of truth.

Now observe also in this portrait of the questioning Christ His penetrating, probing questions that arouse the conscience. He disrobes the thought and lays bare our motives. We really don't want this. Although we like to talk about ourselves, we don't want to get to the bottom of the truth about ourselves. We want to keep it superficial—not too penetrating. In his Nazi prison cell Dietrich Bonhoeffer made the observation that most people "aren't worried about sin." The imprisoned pastor wrote in February of 1944:

"It often fills me with shame here to see how readily men demean themselves just for a bit of gossip, how they prate incessantly about their own private affairs to people who don't deserve it, and

---

[4] Mt. 22:16,17,28,36,42-46 Phillips

who hardly even listen. And the strangest thing about it is that they have no regard whatever for truth; all they want to do is to talk about themselves . . . People here aren't worried about sin, whether their own or anybody else's."[5]

No wonder we express a fear of God. "You speak to us," said the people to Moses when they had heard God speak from Mount Sinai, "you speak to us, but let not God speak to us!"[6] God's word penetrates too deep. God's word probes too far. God's word arouses the conscience, and we shy away from truth! Jesus comes asking questions to prick our conscience:

"A good tree always yields good fruit . . . Can grapes be picked from briars, or figs from thistles?"

He read their thoughts, and said, "Why do you harbour these evil thoughts?"

Again He asked: "Does not the Scripture say, 'My house shall be called a house of prayer for all the nations?' But you have made it a robber's cave."

"How can you have faith so long as you receive honor from one another, and care nothing for the honor that comes from him who alone is God?"[7]

Such questions cut like a newly sharpened knife to the moral quick, and who can answer him a word? They snatch the mask from the hypocrite's face, and our motives lie revealed.

Judas had made all the arrangements. Now he was coming up the mountain to the garden of Gethsemane, leading a group of soldiers. He had gone

[5]Dietrich Bonhoeffer, "Prisoner For God," Macmillan, p. 103
[6]Ex. 20:19 RSV
[7]Mt. 7:16,17; 12:34; Mk. 11:17; Jn. 5:44 English

this far. He was coming to betray Jesus. Still the thoughts kept troubling him. Was he doing right after all? Was he justified in giving Jesus over to the authorities? Yes . . . there was no other way.

There He stands now. The soldiers must stop. He, Judas, will go forward, identify Him, kiss Him. And Jesus asks one question: "Judas, my friend, what made you come here?"[8] Too late. The soldiers come forward. Jesus is taken.

But the question finds its mark. Within hours a remorseful Judas is back in the temple, confronting the priests, throwing the thirty pieces of silver on the marble floor and shouting: "I was wrong—I have betrayed an innocent man to death—I was wrong . . ." They reply coldly: "That's your affair."[9] And Judas goes out to hang himself.

This is surely NOT the purpose of Jesus' probing questions. Jesus arouses the conscience that we may come to Him in confession. He arouses the conscience so that we may discover our guilt complex is guilt as well as complex, and that guilt can be removed by God. If instead of hanging himself, Judas had gone to the cross, he would have heard Jesus' words of forgiveness: "Father, forgive them; for they know not what they do."[10] And that may have covered him.

For Jesus arouses the conscience that we may stop rationalizing and excusing ourselves, and see the truth about sin—the world's sin and my sin—at the

8Mt. 26:50 Phillips
9Mt. 27:4 Phillips
10Lk. 23:34

Cross! Is there any awakening so terrible as that? But Jesus meant it to happen. If we do not think seriously about our sins, it means we have never really been to the Cross! For this is what sin did. And this is where sin can be forgiven.

The questioning Christ also appeals to our emotions. The emotions are not his only court of appeal, but who can deny that emotions are involved in decision? Bunyan says that "Christ seeks entrance not only through Ear-gate and Eye-gate but through Feel-gate."[11] Feeling is one of the gates into the fortress I call "me." Emotion is part of my total personality. The intellect does not function without feeling.

The scientist can become emotional when he makes a sudden discovery or when he lectures on his favorite subject. We have all carried our emotions to a football game, or been moved by a movie. Besides, a man may only discover certain things about a woman when he becomes emotionally involved with her. Some knowledge can be gained by anyone, but only he who falls in love with her discovers her.

Christianity offers a relationship with God. How can God be discovered until our emotions are involved? How can anyone think about God, His beauty, His purity, His majesty, His love—without feeling? "The wonder of God's love produces emotion, or else it is no wonder . . . No great decision in human life is ever made without emotion."[12]

And how do we enter this relationship with God? By faith, prayer, and love. Faith is an emotion. Faith

[11]John Bunyan, "The Holy War"
[12]Bryan Green, "The Practice of Evangelism," Scribner, p. 107

is a response to the God Who reveals Himself. Faith produces a relationship with God, involves us with Him. So the questioning Christ stirs us to faith.

Two blind men follow Him, crying out for mercy and healing. "Do you believe I can do it?" He asks them. "Yes, Lord," they reply. He touches their eyes and heals them.

A man lay with an illness for thirty-eight years, and when Jesus sees him He asks: "Do you want to get well again?" And He brings him to health.

Lazarus has died and Jesus attempts to stir Martha to faith: "I Myself am the Resurrection and the Life. The man who believes in Me will live even though he dies . . . Can you believe that?"[13] Faith involves our emotions. Faith is our response to God.

Prayer is an emotion. Prayer is a relationship with God, a contact felt by the soul. So Jesus tells the story of a farmer who has gone to bed early and is rudely awakened in the middle of the night by a violent knocking on the door and a voice crying: "Friend, lend me three loaves!" And from his warm, cozy upstairs bed the farmer answers:

"Trouble me not: the door is now shut, and my children are with me in bed; I cannot rise . . . " The knocking continues. The farmer, disgruntled, struggles out of bed, grabs a light, goes down to the kitchen, picks out some bread, throws open the door, and shoves the bread into the waiting arms.

"Thank you."

"You're welcome." The door bangs shut, the

---

[13]Mt. 9:28; Jn. 5:6; 11:25,26 Phillips

farmer climbs back upstairs into bed, but the neighbor's persistency has paid off . . . He has the bread!

Then come the questions of Jesus to move us into a relationship with God through prayer:

"If a son shall ask bread of any of you that is a father, will he give him a stone? Or if he ask a fish, will he for a fish give him a serpent? Or if he shall ask an egg, will he offer him a scorpion? If ye then, being evil, know how to give good gifts unto your children; how much more shall your heavenly Father give the Holy Spirit to them that ask him?"[14]

Christianity offers a relationship with God. And how can such a relationship be established without faith and prayer and love—which are all emotions? Our whole personality is involved when we decide. By the feel-gate Jesus would enter our lives. "Do you believe I can do it?"

He aims at the mind, arouses the conscience, appeals to the emotions, and finally assails the will. Here we make our choice. Here we reach a verdict. And reach a verdict we must. When intellectually convinced, conscientiously aroused, emotionally involved, we must choose.

"Who do you say that I am?" "What is your opinion of Christ?" "For what good is it for a man to gain the whole world at the price of his own soul? What could a man offer to buy back his soul once he had lost it?"[15]

The good life, more creature comforts, longer holidays, more money to spend, these possessions

[14]Lk. 11:5-13
[15]Mt. 16:15,26; 22:42 Phillips

and pleasures fill our daily horizon. What remedy is there for this suffocating materialism, but the recovery of a vibrant, vital faith? We are created by God a living soul. The object of life is the development and the redemption of that soul, to find a faith to live by, and a hope worth living for. Suffocating materialism or faith? What is your soul worth? Can anything be worth exchanging it for? Choose. Decide. What if you gain the world and lose your soul?

A disaster occurs in Siloam. A tower falls, killing eighteen; eighteen innocent people. Jesus capitalizes on the headlines: "The eighteen people who were killed when the tower fell on them at Siloam—do you imagine they were more guilty than all the other people living in Jerusalem? I tell you they were not; but unless you repent, you will all of you come to the same end."[16] Decide now. Repent.

Jesus does not mean that we will be attacked by hoodlums, caught in a falling elevator, or killed in an airplane crash, but we will come to a similar end—an even more untimely and unhappy end—at the very end of life. And only repentance can change that ending. Decide now.

"Every time you make a choice," says C. S. Lewis, "you are turning the central part of you that chooses, into something a little different from what it was before. And taking your life as a whole with all your innumerable choices, all your life long you are slowly turning this central thing either into a heavenly creature or into a hellish creature."[17]

[16]Lk. 13:4,5 English
[17]C. S. Lewis, "Christian Behavior," p. 23

The questions of Jesus, sharp as an arrow, aimed with precision, reach their mark: the mind, the conscience, the emotions, the will. And our answers to His questions determine our destiny, for "the Kingdom of Heaven is like a king who arranged a wedding for his son . . . "

The King prepares a banquet. He wants us to be His guests. He sends out an invitation, and with that invitation He provides the proper wedding clothes.

Then the wedding day comes. The guests arrive. There enters a man not properly dressed. They ask him why he is dressed like that? Did he not get an invitation? Yes, he received an invitation, in fact, "I was asked to come, so I came." Why then did he not put on the proper wedding clothes? Did he not receive the clothes with the invitation? Yes, he received the clothes, but was it really necessary for him to wear them? Was it not far more important that he was here and had accepted the invitation? After all, the King did invite him. "I was asked to come, so I came."

Just then the king arrives. And that is what they have all been waiting for, to *see* the king! A hushed silence falls over the assembly. And the king spots the man not properly dressed. "How did you come in here, my friend," he asks, "without being properly dressed for the wedding?" The man stumbles about for words, but can find none. "Tie him up and throw him into darkness outside. He can weep and gnash his teeth there!"[18]

You cannot presume on God's invitation! You

18Mt. 22:1-13 Phillips

cannot come shamelessly with your sins still on you. You must humble yourself. You cannot seat yourself at the banquet table with a dirty shirt and dirty hands. The others washed up! The others dressed up! You exploited the invitation. Your invitation is cancelled when you play a little game with the **grace** of God! The question of the King will stop you . . .

The King of the universe invites you: "Blessed are they who are called unto the marriage supper of the Lamb."[19] He provides the clothing: "They have washed their robes and made them white in the blood of the Lamb."[20] But the greatest truth of all is that this King is waiting for you at a wedding feast! So, what will you answer the questioning Christ today?

[19]Rev. 19:9
[20]Rev. 7:14

CHAPTER 9

THE PRAYING JESUS

"Lord, teach us to pray" (Lk. 11:1)

He was a gifted Preacher, a powerful Person, a Man who drew people to Himself, yet search as you will, His disciples never ask Jesus how to preach or how to become a magnetic person. But they do ask Him: "Lord, teach us to pray." Somehow they realized that behind that magnetic and productive life lay a power unknown to them, a source untapped by them.

They had seen Him get up early in the morning. They had known Him to stay up late at night. They knew He prayed as the need arose. More than once they caught Him in meditation. "Lord, teach us to pray." We, too, want to know the secret of a productive life. We, too, want to tap the source of power.

Today we live in a post-Kantian era. We are persuaded by reason and rational processes. To pray?— Wasted effort. What good does it do? Our world is hard but real; prayer does not help. We get things done by doing, by organizing committees, by governmental action. Write your congressman. Organize a committee. Enforce legislation. Clean up your own street. These are facts. Prayer is wasted motion. Besides, we have prayed for something and it did not happen anyway. We could not change God's purpose. Even a theologian can say that for God to answer prayer is "primitive superstition" and intellectually unacceptable. But if Bultmann is right, Jesus is wrong.

We cannot escape one great truth in Scripture. The men of the Bible prayed. They believed God. Jesus prayed. Jesus believed God. No matter what the climate of the world in which we live, no matter what the temper of the modern mind, no matter what the cold reasoning of the intellectual, there stands in the midst of our gospels this unusual request—a request to know the secret of Jesus' life: "Lord, teach us to pray."

Now, when we think of the praying Christ, many of us hold in our minds a most familiar picture, a picture which has unquestionably a certain beauty about it. This is the picture of Jesus praying in the garden of Gethsemane, seen in many churches. I would not wish to destroy any inspiration a person may have received from it, but the next time you see it, notice something. A halo is about Jesus' head. Light streams in from above. He looks up serene and calm. The picture looks very holy, but it is not very real.

The halo makes Jesus different from us! So does the light. We have no halos. We are ordinary people. We have no light streaming at us from above, not in that way. Prayer for us is effort, exertion, struggle. Was it not that for Jesus? What actually happened in Gethsemane when He sweat as it were great drops of blood, was that not struggle? Effort? He had no halo! The moment Jesus receives a halo and light, He is no longer the human Jesus of the gospels. We destroy the whole gospel story. We deny that Jesus is man, actually man, so completely man that He *needs* to pray! "In the days of his flesh . . . He offered up prayers and supplications with strong crying and tears . . . "[1]

Coleridge well asked the question:

"Why need He pray, who held by filial right,
    O'er all the world alike of thought and sense,
    The fulness of his Sire's omnipotence?
Why crave in prayer what was his own by might?
Vain is the question,—Christ was man in need,
And being man his duty was to pray.
The son of God confess'd the human need,
And doubtless ask'd a blessing every day."[2]

So we see Him leaving His place of rest early in the morning, even before sun-up, to pray. He seeks to be alone with God, to listen, to request, to enter conversation, to receive guidance, to know the Eternal, to see the Light, to obey His Father. Such prayer is not escape. He prepares Himself for the day's work. The tempo of the day is so hectic, He must meet it with the right temper. And that means He cannot squeeze God in just anywhere, but He makes planned times for Him . . .

At night Jesus prays. Late, when the work is over and most of us enjoy our television, the figure of

[1]Heb. 5:7
[2]"Masterpieces of Religious Verse" edited by James Dalton Morrison, p. 212

Jesus enters that solitude again. Evidently the pressures of life are so overwhelming, the temptations so strong, the problems so vast, the burdens so heavy, He must take this time; and three times the gospels record that Jesus spends the whole night in prayer.

This closeness with His heavenly Father prepares Him for the crises in His life. When, for example, He comes to the grave of Lazarus, He is able to say: "I thank Thee that Thou hast heard me, Father. And I knew that Thou hearest me always."[3] He can raise the dead because He has prayed. He is fully obedient to God, and therefore powers that cannot be entrusted to another human being are given to Him. Prayer is the key to His power. His disciples know it: "Lord, teach us to pray." There is really no other explanation.

Jesus realizes that He is now only an instrument through which the power of God flows. This awakens His need to pray. Only an instrument.

Nor should we fail to notice that He who prayed early, late, and in crisis times, also prays at the height of His success. Even then He remembers His dependence upon God. Great crowds throng Him, multitudes come for help and healing, but He withdraws Himself into the wilderness and prays. Jesus knows that He cannot continue as an instrument of God's power at the height of His success without solitude. Therefore He practices what He preaches: "When you pray, go into a room by yourself, shut the door, and pray to your Father who is there in the secret place."[4] His room includes the wilderness, the

[3]Jn. 11:41,42
[4]Mt. 6:6 English

desert, the mountain, the woods, and wherever quiet can be found . . . quiet and God.

We dare not assume that these were the only times He prayed. For Jesus prayer was constant. His life was His prayer and His prayer was His life. Prayer and life cannot be separated. Prayer does not belong in a compartment whether in the morning or at night. Like breathing, prayer was always part of Him.

To us prayer becomes sometimes (to use the picturesque phrase of Helmut Thielecke) an attempt to "cover our rear." A kind of insurance policy, a safety device, by which we make sure nothing will happen. We want to impress God with our prayers, so that we may be covered in case something should happen to go wrong. As we advance through life, we want to "cover our rear." For Jesus, prayer is no such insurance; prayer is life.

But what did He pray about? What did He pray for? The longest prayer by Jesus, recorded in Scripture, surely gives us insight into His prayer-concern. He prays for the glory of God: "Father, glorify thy Son, that thy Son also may glorify Thee . . . I have manifested Thy name . . ."[5]

God is at work in Jesus. Jesus has brought God to men. Eternal life consists in knowing the Father and the Son. That God may be known, that Christ Himself may be recognized as the Eternal One who has entered time, as the Word made flesh, that this incarnation may be accepted, for this He prays. This is no selfish prayer. This prayer underlies His mission

[5]Jn. 17:1,6

104

and His whole purpose in coming to earth. Since He is the revealer of the only God, since He is the One who has come from eternity, then "Father, glorify Thou me with thine own self with the glory which I had with Thee before the world was."[6]

The world lives in superstition. The world is ignorant of this truth. May truth be proclaimed! May God in Jesus Christ, whom Thou hast sent, be made known! So may men be brought from death to eternal life.

Of course, Jesus prays about Himself, too. In this prayer He accepts the will of God. He prepares for the cross. He speaks to God as His Father, whom He loves and trusts, even as a very young child will completely trust his father. Again Jesus practices what He preaches to us. He tells us that unless we become as little children, we cannot enter the kingdom of God. He comes as a little child Himself in prayer, believing.

And here we must learn something important about prayer. We never hear Jesus pray directly about His temptations and tests. He always thanks God or draws on God's power to overcome the test. In this prayer we do not hear about the ignorance of the world, but about the revelation of truth. We do not find Jesus dwelling on His failure with Judas, but rather on continued strength for the disciples. In other words, Jesus does not, like Adam and Eve, keep thinking of the forbidden fruit they must not eat, but of the God who can keep Him from that

---

[6]Jn. 17:5

forbidden fruit of worry, anxiety, disobedience, and despair.

You can pray in a way that is all wrong. You can keep your eye on the object to be avoided, the forbidden tree, and then run right smack into it! Like the beginning skier who keeps eyeing that tree in his descent, petrified with fear that he will run into it—and does. Perhaps you have a real battle with your passions, and you keep thinking of them while you pray. But you don't want to yield to *that*, and then you think of it again, no, not *that*. Yet all the time these fantasies about *that* are right in the midst of your prayers.

"O Lord, deliver me from my passions.

Thou knowest how I fall so easily.

Keep me from that sin.   Amen."

That is not prayer. By concentrating on these passions you have actually made them stronger. You have held their image before you, and the net result is worse, instead of better. And you have not achieved what you hoped to accomplish.

"O Lord, Thou art in me, and all power is Thine!

I thank Thee that Thou hast heard me.

Thou dost hear me always.

May the love wherewith Thou hast loved me,
be in me.   Amen."

Does that sound more like Jesus praying? It should.[7] God is positive. Jesus' prayers for Himself are positive affirmations of truth. This is the right way to pray. Don't dwell on the passions but on the power that will overcome them.

---

[7]See Jn. 11:41,42; 17:21,26

Of course Jesus prayed for others. For their understanding: "I have given them thy word . . . Sanctify them through thy truth: thy word is truth."[8] For their love: May "they be made perfect in one . . ." and may "the love wherewith Thou hast loved me be in them."[9] Truth—the badge of distinction. Love —the bond of unity. There is moral power when truth unites with love. Only then will the world believe.

There will always be tests: "The world hath hated them, because they are not of the world . . . I pray . . . that Thou shouldest keep them from the evil."[10] And Jesus, with eyes on His Father, prays for our safekeeping in the trials of life. "Simon, Simon, take heed: Satan has been given leave to sift all of you like wheat; but for you I have prayed that your faith may not fail . . ."[11] prayed for your *faith*!

Jesus prays because He believes. He really believes that God will hear. He really believes that God will act in these apostles' lives. He believes He lives in a friendly universe, because He knows God as His Father. He knows that His Father will offer His Son for man's sin. This is how He knows that "God is love." This is why He prays with confidence.

Therefore, too, He can climb the holy mountain of prayer and say with perfect assurance: "Not my will, but thine, be done."[12] Here He reaches the heights, for this is no prayer of resignation, as if He sits back and says to the God of the universe:

[8]Jn. 17:14,17
[9]Jn. 17:23,26
[10]Jn. 17:14,15
[11]Lk. 22:31,32 English
[12]Lk. 22:42

"Whatever happens was bound to happen anyhow." No, first He has asked and petitioned. He has come humbly as a child to his father. Indeed, He has sweat as it were drops of blood! Now He can say: "Not my will, but thine, be done."

Don't begin prayers by saying: "Whatever happens was bound to happen anyhow." Then you can never really pray. That is not faith. But at the end, when you have made your requests, believe that God will choose what is right from these childish prayers, even as a father on earth sorts out his children's requests. Everything a child asks is not granted, but only what is good. So at the end say: "Thy will be done," which means, "Thou knowest what I really need, and I believe that Thou wilt give me what is just and good. Amen."

And now I come to the reason for the portrait of the praying Christ. If Jesus Christ, the Son of God, the Eternal Word made human flesh, took time to pray early in the morning, late at night, sometimes all night, at the times of crisis, and even at the height of His success; if Jesus Christ often sought out the solitary place, the desert, the mountain, the woods, or Galilean sea, to pray for God's glory, His own mission, His disciples' faith, and His own testings, how much more need we who are miserable, burdened, anxious, faithless, tempted, weak and powerless human creatures. PRAY! He has given us an example, that we should follow in His steps.

"The man who prays (not the man who works only, but the man who prays) is the man who stays awake, who does not dream and confuse the big things with the small things, but retains a wide-awake and realistic sense of the real proportions of life. The man who prays knows that there is only one thing that really counts and that is getting straight with God. The man who prays also loses the anxiety of life because he knows that . . . history will end according to plan, and that nothing can happen to us except what He has foreseen, and what is for our good."[13]

The praying Christ shows us our need to pray to a Father who hears.

"Lord, teach us to pray."

[13]Helmut Thielecke, "Christ and The Meaning of Life," Harper, p. 95

CHAPTER 10

THE DISTURBING JESUS

*"The last shall be first,
and the first last" (Mt. 20:16)*

Do we really know what we are talking about when we speak of "an experience of God?" Are we aware what we are saying, what we claim for ourselves, when we use the word "God?" Could it be that "an experience of God" has come to mean merely something comforting and peaceful, something wonderfully soothing? Our continual emphasis (in the West) on "peace"—peace of mind, peace of soul, peace with God—may create a picture of restfulness, a kind of foggy feeling which settles over a person. The emphasis (in the East) on "mysticism" fabricates a blissful union with the Infinite, a suspended floating in space between time and eternity.

What really takes place in "an experience of God?" No doubt there may be peace, bliss, joy. But is that all? Before any so-called comfortable feeling must there not be something agonizing, uprooting, disturbing? Before the joy of the babe come the birth pangs. To enter God's presence is actually disturbing.

When Jacob pillowed his head on a stone in the desert, he had a dream. He saw a ladder which reached to heaven. He heard God's voice. When he awoke he found himself in a cold sweat: "Surely the Lord is in this place; and I knew it not ... How dreadful is this place!"[1]

When Isaiah entered the temple, God gave him such an experience of His holiness that the prostrate prophet cried out: "Woe is me! for I am undone; for I am a man of unclean lips."[2] "Scripture," says John Calvin, "represents saints always impressed and disturbed on every discovery of God." And how can it be otherwise?

God is holy. We are unholy. God is light. We are darkness. He is righteous. We are sinners. When we who are what we are dare to approach Him Who is what He is, there is a revealing, a purging, and resultant confession. God disturbs us simply by what He is. No experience of God can be genuine, if it is not disturbing. And if we know anything about Jesus, we can never again see a soft, kindly God who covers everything with His mantle of forgiveness, but only a holy God who demands a cross to deal with sin.

Small wonder then, when God becomes Man and walks among us, He disturbs. We cannot avoid the portrait of the disturbing Christ. Jesus refers to Himself as bread men must eat to have life eternal, and asks: "Does this shock you?"[3] It did.

His vigorous teaching on the corruption of human

---

[1]Gen. 28:16,17
[2]Isa. 6:5
[3]Jn. 6:61 English

nature brings the disciples to Him with the question: "Do you know that the Pharisees have taken great offense at what you have been saying?"[4] They did.

Jesus never neutralizes. "There was a division therefore again . . . for these sayings."[5] "He that is not with Me, is against Me."[6] He antagonizes the proud; He attracts the humble. He alienates those who will not be disturbed. He receives the adoration of all who will enter the agonizing experience He offers—the experience of new birth.

When Peter awakes to this Person who is with him in the boat, he falls on his knees: "Go, Lord, leave me, sinner that I am!" Every weakness, every failure, every transgression known to Christ! Every subterfuge, every camouflage, every pretense at respectability, pierced by the Light. With a scorching sense of shame he sees himself for what he is: "Leave me, sinner that I am!"[7]

Comfortable? I think not. Jesus stings and hurts and disturbs before healing. A violent uprooting occurs before obedient discipleship. "Do not be afraid," said Jesus . . . "From now on you will be catching men."[8] But we will not obey unless we see our need to obey! We will not follow Him until we lose our self-reliance.

And this is precisely the reason why Jesus comes to disturb us. We have a high opinion of ourselves. We identify ourselves with everything that is good,

[4]Mt. 15:12 English
[5]Jn. 10:19
[6]Mt. 12:30
[7]Lk. 5:8 English
[8]Lk. 5:8-10 English

and immediately disregard anything ugly. Have I had a bad dream last night? Oh, but I'm not that hateful person I dreamed about. This is not me. I don't act like that monster. I am not that lustful, that low. No, that is all something else. That is not me. It was just a bad dream.

In the course of a day I receive a compliment. Someone tells me I am very generous or kind. I thank him, and deny it. But inwardly I know he is right! In fact, I am far better than he has any idea of! If he really knew me, he would realize how extremely generous and kind I am.

I have a terrible tendency to identify myself with everything that is good: "This is what I am." Whatever may incriminate me, I reject: "I am not like that." I tend to go about feeling that my goodness is quite sufficient to impress people—even God. Yes, in the end I will impress even God with my good life. I am kind; I help my neighbors. I am generous; I give to the Community Chest. I am good enough; why should *I* have to go to Church? Let me say it: "What more should I do than I am now doing?"

Into that very satisfactory world I have created for myself, Jesus means to say: "What you really think you are, you are not. What you do not think you are, that is the real you." He turns me around. "You have learned that our forefathers were told, 'Do not commit murder; anyone who commits murder must be brought to judgment.' But what I tell you is this: Anyone who nurses anger against his brother must be brought to judgment; If he abuses his brother he must answer for it to the court; if he sneers at him he will have to answer for it in the fire of hell."[9]

And I, who never thought of myself as a murderer, I am now told that the seeds of hatred lodge within me. Perhaps it all reflects in my dreams anyway. The same is true for adultery, stealing, lying, coveting, and all the other evils I thought I had scrupulously avoided. Jesus is far too disturbing. But how else can I find out that I need a Saviour? How else can I know He comes to restore me to God? How else can I fathom the need for the Cross? I, too, cry out: "Go, Lord, leave me, sinner that I am!" But I am thankful He will not. He has come to save me and call me to obedience.

Now that is only the beginning. All through our Christian lives Jesus will disturb us. I used to think when someone becomes a Christian he must submit to the traditional picture. He must "fit in" with all the rest of us. He must be labelled "Christian," so that anyone can recognize him as a Christian. Every Christian must look and act alike, and be as easily recognizable as the same company cans on the supermarket shelf. He has to conform to a certain size can. Some things he can do, other things he cannot; some thou shalts, and quite a few thou shalt nots.

Of course, he must give up his "worldly habits" and "worldly friends," and if, for example, he still drinks or smokes, he will not quite fit into the can. We will have to compress him a little further. So, all of my Christianity reduces itself to one long exercise

---

[9]Mt. 5:21,22 English

of compressing and squeezing into a can labelled, "Christian."

But I can't find anything about this in your words, Lord . . . Nothing about a canned Christian. You never bound your disciples. You set them free. You told us to deny ourselves, but You said it in the positive context of following. You strike at the core of our pride. You do not want us to chop off a few habits and then sneak that core of pride into the can. How subtle and sinful we are! You have come to release us; not to repress us. You have come to set us free. "If then the Son sets you free, you will indeed be free."[10]

Besides, I thought that all we have to do is build a Church, preach the gospel, sing a few hymns, and then people will flock to us. We'll hold a tea and the neighborhood ladies will come. We'll serve ice cream and all the youth will come running. That's all we have to do. Pray, give, worship, and socialize. We can send out missionaries to other countries to convert the heathen for us. That is the traditional way. We have been doing it for years.

But I can't find anything in Your words to substantiate this, Jesus. Nothing. You never said people should come to us. You did say that we should go to them. You never told us anything about socials, but quite a bit about prayer. You never said others should become missionaries for us. You said we all have the privilege of being your witnesses. Did You, in fact, ever tell me anything else but to pray and witness, and that You would be with me? Have I

[10]Jn. 8:36 English

117

fallen so far into my comfortable churchy pattern that I cannot hear your disturbing voice any more?

A couple was travelling in Alaska by dogsled. It was 40° below. He walked with the dog team, while she sat comfortably on the sled. He kept an eye on her and noticed her beginning to doze. Suddenly he took hold of the sled, jarred it violently, shook her off, and drove the dogs on. She woke up and called out. He did not stop. She picked herself up, started running, calling all the while. Half a mile later he stopped the sled. She climbed aboard, visibly annoyed, but she didn't say a word. They arrived home. She could not contain herself any longer: "Why did you do that to me?" "Because," he said, "if you had fallen asleep, you would have frozen to death."

You begin to see why Jesus must disturb us. We have grown content with ourselves, satisfied in our thinking, traditional in our practices. He must shake us loose. And if He is the Lord, the Word made flesh, the Light in the midst of our darkness, He must show us reality behind the appearance of things. Our values are so irrelevant. He must establish totally different standards for us.

"Believe me, a rich man will find it very difficult to enter the Kingdom of Heaven. Yes, I repeat, a camel could more easily squeeze through the eye of a needle than a rich man get into the Kingdom of God." That the values of the disciples are turned topsy-turvy by that remark is obvious from their question: "Then who can possibly be saved?"[11]

---

[11]Mt. 19:23-25 Phillips

118

According to Jesus a rich man can end in torment while a beggar finds salvation. Those who exalt themselves shall be humbled, and the humble exalted. The first shall be last and the last, first. Everything is turned upside down! And we thought we were driving our car in high, while we were in reverse all the time. . . . The high low; the rich poor; the first last; the low high? the poor rich? the last first? What is this? This is confusing. This is too radical!

It reverses everything we have lived for. This reveals what lies behind our phony appearances. The funeral of the rich man was probably held in grand style attended by scores of mourners. They filed past the exquisite casket almost lost amid countless beautiful and expensive sprays. The beggar may have been buried on state funds or by the kind-heartedness of the mortician. But all that means nothing. We bestow honors where God may be silent. We may be silent where angels sing praise. The first shall be last, and the last. . . .first!

"Unfair, Dad, it's terribly unfair," he said to his father on that eventful day. "I have served you. For years I have served you. I never wandered away. I have been obedient, industrious, reliable. You know how I have worked on the farm ever since I was so high. Even when I was married I only took three days off. I've never taken much of a vacation.

"And this brother of mine . . . You remember the day he asked for his money, his share? Yes, I know you remember! And you gave it all to him. So what did he do? He beat it out of here, to God knows where, and he lived it up. I mean, he really lived it up. You know what he did. You were young once yourself. He spent it all on women and wine and while he was having a good time, what was I doing? Working. Working on your farm. Nothing but work.

"Now he's come back. Your son has come home. Why? Because he ran out of money, that's why. He was living in a pigpen. And what do you do? You throw a big feast. You kill the fatted calf—the one we saved for the holidays next month. You know how I've been working to fatten her up. But you have to serve up a first-rate roast for this fun-loving son of yours.

"Well, I won't come to your party. I can't do it, Dad. My wife and I—we just can't join you tonight. You see, Father, never, never once, *never* did you give me a real party. I don't understand you, Father. You're acting mighty strange now that your son is back. You don't seem like my Father at all. And I've worked for you all my life. . . ."

"My son, you have been with me all the time and everything I have is yours. But we *had* to celebrate and show our joy. For this is your brother; I thought he was dead—and he's alive. I thought he was lost—and he is found!"[12]

This is exactly what the disturbing Christ comes to tell us Christians. We trust in our achievements. We have worked hard. We have been obedient. We like the way everything appears. We must have gained some credit with our heavenly Father. We have been moral and religious. We can't just throw that all aside as if it doesn't count! We cannot join

---

[12]Lk. 15:31,32 Phillips

this feast for a prodigal son. This is not why we have been good and moral. We have not been religious for nothing.

The whole scheme of things is unfair. Yes, even God seems unfair. Because if it really is this way with God, we should have gotten *our* money and had *our* kicks. Why not? If you can always return and have a feast? Why waste all your life on God's farm? Why be good when you can live it up and then come back and repent?

No—the real values of life cannot be like that. It just cannot be. God is for those who are good and religious, who worship and pray, who fit into the pious cans, who trust and obey. The first shall be first and the last shall be last! God was mighty lucky when he got us. He made a good choice.

And this is how our very goodness can keep us from God. Our very spirituality can rob us of the Spirit. The rich cannot enter the kingdom. The rich who trust in goods and goodness, in achievements of the self; who fail to see a brother in every prodigal over whom our Father rejoices.

All of this Jesus finally wraps up in a discomforting parable, which also takes place on a farm. At daybreak the owner hires some workers and offers to pay them a regular day's pay. They agree and go to work. At nine he goes to town and sees a few men in the park and asks them if they want work. They do, and join the others on the farm. About noon he finds others and signs them for a half day. It happens again around three and even at five while the sun prepares to slip over the horizon.

At six the men line up for their pay. First come those who have only worked an hour. But, what is this? They are given a whole day's pay? For one hour's work? They are sure glad they went to work. Their only regret is that they did not go out sooner. They can hardly believe the generosity of the owner. Those who went to work at three also receive a full day's pay. This is great! They don't deserve it, but they're not about to quarrel. They go happily on their way and so do most of the others.

Last of all arrive those who worked the full day. "There is something fishy going on here," they say to themselves as they are paid the same. "Something is not right. Yes, we agreed on a day's wages, but if these others could get it for one hour, surely we are entitled to more? Wait till the union hears about this! We had to stand in that long pay line, and we're being paid last, and we went to work first! It isn't fair. Something is not right!"

"The owner turned to one of them and said: 'My friend, I am not being unfair to you. You agreed on the usual wage for the day, did you not? Take your pay and go home. I choose to pay the last man the same as you. Surely I am free to do what I like with my own money. Why be jealous because I am kind?' "[13]

It is as if Jesus says to us: "You will have to understand that this world is a farm. It isn't yours, but God's. It all belongs to Him. You only work here.

"When God calls you to work for Him, you had

[13]Mt. 20:13-15 English

122

better go. If He comes to you early in life, obey Him. Put your hand to the plow and don't look back. If He comes to you in the middle of life, heed His voice. Serve Him. Don't worry about your wasted years. Just go. And even if He should come to you in the closing moments of your earthly pilgrimage, He calls you to enter the farm. It's not too late. It's never too late. Obey His voice. That is what counts *now*.

"And when payday comes. . . . If you have just recently gone to work for God, yours will be the greatest joy of all. You will receive eternal life, even you, even though you repented in the twilight years. Your only regret will be that you did not enter sooner into the joy of service.

Did you work the whole day? You have been a Christian since your early teens? Eternal life is yours. The Kingdom of God. That's what you bargained for, isn't it? That's what you went out to serve Him for, isn't it? Then be content with what belongs to you. It really does belong to you now.

Don't criticize. Don't keep looking at all these others whom God also allows in. Perhaps you think they don't belong with you? You have been a good church member all your life? If you criticize, you won't find yourself in the Kingdom at all. You will not want to sit down to the feast the Father has planned. And you can be sure that He has planned a feast. The first shall be last, and the last first."

So, if we are to have a genuine experience of God, He will disturb us. He will jar us loose from our comfortable neat patterns. Things cannot remain as they are. Jesus is the disturber. But . . . some workers are more than content with their pay. No wonder: they did not deserve it. The boy who comes home receives a joyous welcome. He knows he doesn't deserve it either.

The pain of new birth brings the joy of fulfillment. In the midst of an experience that made him agonize and confess, Pascal cries out: "Joy, joy, joy, tears of joy!" C. S. Lewis entitles his painful conversion: "Surprised by Joy." The disturbing Christ brings joy. But agony before ecstasy. Uprooting before settling. Suffering and trial before everlasting peace.

And Jesus asks: "Does this shock you?" It should!

CHAPTER 11

THE FEARLESS JESUS

"My house shall be called the house of prayer; but ye have made it a den of thieves" (Mt. 21:13)

"And Jesus went into the temple of God, and cast out all them that sold and bought in the temple, and overthrew the tables of the moneychangers, and the seats of them that sold doves, and said unto them, It is written, My house shall be called the house of prayer; but ye have made it a den of thieves."[1]

What have we here? Can it be so? A picture of Jesus in the temple chasing out the moneychangers with a whip in His hand? Is this the singing poet who speaks of the birds of the air and the lilies of the field? Is this the homespun philosopher who tells stories about a woman baking bread or fishermen hauling in a catch? Is this the gentle Man from Nazareth who helps those the world passes by, and holds little children in His arms? Yes!

You have known it from the moment you entered the gallery. This portrait of the fearless Christ immediately attracted your eye. Its vividness and bold-

[1]Mt. 21:12,13

ness caught your attention. You could hardly wait to look at it closely.

And now you can see Him who dares to enter the sacred temple with the authority of God. Now you can behold the hucksters and traders falling over each other to escape the fire in His eyes, as the money rolls out of their greedy grasp. Now you can see the animals scurrying and doves fluttering away. Now you can see priests and scribes standing by unable to move, gaping in utter amazement at the scene, shocked by the daring of this Galilean. Now you can see Jesus appear with the whip in His hands, gripping it tight with whited knuckles; His jaw set, determined, His face aflame with the holiness of God. "It is written, My house shall be called the house of prayer; but ye have made it a den of thieves."

Does it surprise you that this portrait hangs in the exhibit? It should not. Jesus was a Prophet, too. He inherited the great prophetic tradition. He had the boldness of those who spoke God's word to man fearlessly.

"Who do people say the Son of Man is?"

"Some say. . . .one of the prophets."[2]

Would it not follow that the greatest of the prophets performs the most heroic of all prophetic deeds?

This fearless act flows from His constant revelation of God. Jesus combines in His person the goodness and the severity of God. A holy God must cleanse an unholy temple. A holy God demands a

[2]Mt. 16:13,14

holy people. He who taught quietly on a mountain-side in Galilee also cleansed the great temple in Jerusalem! He comes in the name of His Father. He is courageous because He knows whose kingdom He brings. He is not afraid because He believes in holiness and truth.

Now, it should be obvious that this cleansing of the temple was a symbolic act. He did in reality drive out the moneychangers. But what He really attacks is the religion of the times. The cleansing of the temple is an outward act which shows the far greater need of cleansing religious thought and worship. What Jesus is really after appears in the most fearless sermon of holy Scripture, which He preaches immediately after the temple episode—a sermon preached in the great prophetic tradition, which penetrates the masks of hypocrisy and lays bare a wrong approach to God.

"The Scribes and the Pharisees teach the Mosaic Law, so you must do what they tell you and follow their instructions. But you must not imitate their lives! For they preach and do not practice . . . You Scribes and Pharisees, play-actors that you are!. . . . You say, 'If anyone swears by the Temple it doesn't count, but if he swears by the gold of the Temple he is bound by his oath.' You blind idiots, which is the more important, the gold or the Temple which sanctifies the gold?"[3]

They were clever, but without principle: a man makes a vow to God. He fails to keep it. This is not so serious, "to err is human." He has brought his

[3]Mt. 23:2,3,13,16,17 Phillips

gift, and the gift has been accepted. He has made his oath by the altar, but that will not be held against him. The religion Jesus exposes has become slick, instead of spiritual.

I am told a current practice in the confessional is to confess all one's sins to the priest except those of which a person is really ashamed.

The priest then asks: "Have you completed your confession?"

"Yes, father."

A pause. "Oh, I forgot; I told a lie."

That lie is the one just now told to cover the sins one is ashamed to confess. The priest then absolves the confessor without having heard a full confession.

Religious practice can become slick for those who may not believe in such a confessional. Jesus tells us we should not be anxious about tomorrow or burden ourselves by worry and care, for we have a Father in heaven who will take care of us. But we go right on in our fretfulness and anxiety, develop ulcers and tense nerves, and blandly say: "You can't change human nature." And still we believe in God.

Jesus tells us we are the salt of the earth. Therefore we must make contact with and flavor the society in which we live. But we remain in the saltshakers of our Christian circles, and leave witnessing to the world to the minister. Yet all the while we think we are the salt of the earth. Mercury has a tendency to escape the pressure of human touch. We have a tendency to escape the pressure of the Divine touch. Our religion is slick—not spiritual. A slick religion leads nowhere.

What then is a spiritual faith? Spiritual faith can never be something *we* manipulate but only that which manipulates *us*. God cannot be controlled. He must control us. The grace of God is a gift. It is not wrapped, packaged and given out by us. We do not have hold of the gospel (that's slick religion). The gospel must have hold of us (that becomes spiritual strength).

A spiritual person is open to God. A spiritual person is humble and allows God to move into his life. The wind blows where it will. The wind will not blow where we direct it. God's movement (like wind) is out of man's control. An electric fan can circulate hot air in a room, but that is very different from a fresh breeze outside. When we attempt to manipulate the Spirit of God who would sweep us up into God's activity, our religion becomes the religion of the electric fan. The spiritual man, on the other hand, will be open to the breeze of God's Spirit.

The fearless Christ exposes a slick religion which is not spiritual. "My house shall be called the house of prayer."

But the temple of our lives must also be cleansed of a religion of form which fails to be a force: "You Scribes and Pharisees, you utter frauds! You pay your tithe on mint and anise and cummin, and neglect the things which carry far more weight in the Law—justice, mercy and good faith. These are the things you should have observed—without neglecting the others. You call yourselves leaders, and yet you can't see an inch before your noses. You filter out a mosquito and swallow a camel."[4]

[4]Mt. 23:23,24 Phillips

Forms are so convenient. Laws can tell you what and what not to do. Regulations govern all the facets of religion from worship to food, from tithing to washing. Adhere to them and you will be a "good Christian." So religion is reduced to regulations instead of being a relationship.

What Jesus says is like an amusing comic strip.

Picture 1: A man enters a restaurant.

Picture 2: He is served a bowl of soup.

Picture 3: He calls the waiter back. "Waiter, adjust your bifocals. There's a mosquito in my soup."

Picture 4: The waiter peers down: "Sorry, Sir, I'll get another bowl." The man: "Never mind. Bring the next course."

Picture 5: The waiter leads in a camel.

Last Picture: The man swallows the camel.

Grotesque? But the mosquito was unclean and the camel clean, according to their laws and regulations. A religion of force has become a form. And this is the danger: these forms become the total thrust of religion. Justice, mercy, and faith are all but forgotten.

The story is told of a group of men exploring the Arctic. They huddled about their flickering candles. The temperature dropped so low that the flames froze in mid-air. They broke off these frozen flames and wore them for charms. That which once gave warmth was now mere ornament.

In the frigid atmosphere of a religion of form, we

131

take the flame of the Spirit, attempt to contain it, and adorn ourselves with an orthodox creed.

Jesus came to bring fire on the earth. Wherever the Spirit of God is, the fire falls. It fell on the day of Pentecost. It could fall now—anywhere. For the Spirit comes unannounced as wind. . .

We do it again and again. We satisfy ourselves with beliefs and creeds—creeds about that which is really fire, forms about that which once was force. But no matter how correct and even essential a creed may be, it is not the real thing. . . .We enter a Church, take part in ritual and ceremony, worship and prayer. And after giving an offering and singing our hymns, we depart. This cannot be the end-all of Christianity.

What we narrow down, Jesus widens out. Christianity must become a force . . . a force of justice in a world of injustice; a force of mercy in a merciless society; a force of faith where men live by doubt and despair. The sinner is not a person to be avoided. He is a subject of injustice to be sought out and loved. Mercy is not a form for friends, but a power to demonstrate even to enemies. Faith is no private relationship with God, but an arm which encircles the lost. No wonder the temple must be swept clean of form-religion to make way for the fire of force: "My house shall be called a house of prayer."

Jesus will also cleanse the temple of a religion that is respectable without being renewing. "What miserable frauds you are, you Scribes and Pharisees! You clean the outside of the cup and the dish, while the inside is full of greed and self-indulgence. Can't you see, Pharisee? First, wash the inside of a cup or a plate, and then you can polish the outside. You are like white-washed tombs, which look fine on the outside but inside are full of dead men's bones and all kinds of rottenness. In the same way you appear like good men on the outside—but inside you are a mass of pretence and wickedness."[5]

I do not think people are hypocrites deliberately. Most religious people are sincere. The leaders in Jesus' day were not hypocrites consciously. They were fervent in their desire to please God. Before his conversion Paul was a good, religious person. He was not converted from atheism, irreligion, or an evil life. He was deeply religious. He adhered to good principles and believed in God. He lived according to the tradition of the elders. But a renewal took place in his heart.

What had gone wrong then? When we become so involved with externals there is no time for anything else. It is like this.

You expect guests. You sweep, dust, vacuum, wax, cook, bake, wash, clean, bathe, dress, powder, comb, pamper and perfume yourself, then the doorbell rings. You are ready just in time. Are you ready? Well, the house is respectable and you are dressed to meet your guests. But have you taken any time to think about the meaning of this visit? Have you thought of the real needs of your guests? No; no time for that. You have washed the outside of the cup, so to speak, but have left the coffee ring on the inside.

When we busy ourselves with the externals of

[5]Mt. 23:25-28 Phillips

religion, we have no time for inside changes. All effort goes toward respectability. And we miss the meaning of life—regeneration—the renewal of the heart.

We dare not treat Christianity as we do certain medications, which say on the bottle: "For external use only." Generally another label accompanies that one: "Poison." Christianity externally applied becomes poisonous, indeed.

A respectable appearance makes people think well of us. It brings compliments: "You've got a nice house and you're a good dresser." But who knows what is beneath this veneer of impeccable correctness? Who knows what is beneath my serious demonstrations of devotion? My Sunday best may hide my Monday worst. Respectability? Christianity is not washing a man's hands, but washing his heart. It has nothing to do with acting a part, but with being a new person.

Something has to happen on the inside. With all my pious pretenses at a religious life, I may be haunted by hidden temptations of which no one else knows. How can I overcome them? What can I do about them? Jesus comes not merely to make me respectable on the outside, but to give me a new heart on the inside; to renew me by a new Spirit— the Holy Spirit—and change the direction of my life. He tells me from my heart proceeds evil. So He must change my heart. I cannot do it. The meaning of Christianity centers *here,* in the heart.

This does not mean I at once become a good person. It means rather that I commit myself to Him who is Good, and that I busy myself with internals and not externals of faith. I must walk with God daily. I must be open to Christ's presence. I must receive His Spirit and Word in my heart. The fearless Christ must cleanse the temple of my life of a mere external, respectable religion, that my heart may be renewed. "My house shall be called a house of prayer."

We are also tempted to enshrine the past and ignore the present: "You build tombs for the prophets, and decorate monuments for good men of the past, and then say, 'If we had lived in the times of our ancestors we should never have joined in the killing of the prophets.' Yes, 'your ancestors'— *that* shows you to be sons, indeed, of those who murdered the prophets. Go ahead then, and finish off what your ancestors tried to do."[6]

Most of us identify ourselves with the great of the past. Who seriously boasts of following in the footsteps of the infamous, in company with Cain, Esau, or Judas? The Pharisees identified themselves with the prophets. Jesus identified them with those who slew the prophets. Their minds were already set on getting rid of Him. They soon reveal by their actions on which side they belong. "You serpents, you viper's brood, how do you think you are going to avoid being condemned . . .?"[7]

We identify ourselves with everything noble in our heritage. We applaud the reformers for their faith. We admire the saints for their holiness. We acclaim the martyrs who lay down their lives for the gospel. We would not class ourselves with those who burned

[6]Mt. 23:29-32 Phillips
[7]Mt. 23:33 Phillips

martyrs at the stake. We are not the descendants of the infamous. We belong in the company of the faithful. We are the front-line defenders of the faith. Jesus certainly upset the front-line defenders of the faith *then*.

This is all so easy. A savage chief heard the story of the crucifixion. "Had I been there," he cried out as he swung his menacing weapon, "I would have cut those wicked . . . into a thousand pieces." But, says David Smith as he tells the story, when the savage chief was asked to forsake his evil ways and give his heart to Christ, he refused.[8]

Something else really concerns Jesus. While we enshrine the past, we may be ignoring the present! What good is it to believe something about Jesus from history, without experience of His power now? What good is orthodox doctrine, if there is no flame of the Spirit now? What good is the profoundest respect for His death and resurrection, if there is no wind sweeping us up into God's activity now? What good is all our biblical historic Christianity, if Jesus is not the same *today* as He was yesterday? Do not ignore today. The living Christ will cast from the temple all religion which merely enshrines the Christian past. The thrust of the gospel is for relevance today.

"Easter Day, April 2nd, 1738. I preached in our College chapel on, 'The hour cometh, and now is, when the dead shall hear the voice of the Son of God . . .' I see the promise; but it is afar off . . . The hour cometh: but, it is afar off . . .'"

---

[8]From David Smith, "The Days of His Flesh," p. 415

Then turn a few pages in John Wesley's Journal. Seven weeks later, Pentecost Sunday, the Spirit blows like a fresh breeze and falls like fire on him. Afar off? "The hour cometh—*and now is!*" John Wesley is changed.

James S. Stewart comments on this inner transformation. "We glorify the past, and say, 'O had I lived in that great day when Christ was really here!' . . . But why dwell regretfully upon an age that is gone? Christ is here! The Lord and Giver of life is here. The hour cometh—and now is!

'Today, if ye will hear His voice, harden not your heart.' Today reach out hands of faith, and pray, 'Jesus, think on me! Thou ever-present Saviour, whose name is Resurrection and life, speak with the voice that wakes the dead: shatter the silence, pierce the gloom of my lost worthless soul.' And He will work in you the everlasting miracle, the mightiest of all His mighty acts: and you will . . . live!"[9]

Let Jesus cleanse the temple of your life. "Have you forgotten that your body is the temple of the Holy Spirit, who lives in you?"[10] Let Him cast out all that smacks of being slick but is not spiritual; all religion of form which is hardly a force; external respectability which fails to renew the heart; and all that would enshrine the past while ignoring the present. If only you will let Him sweep you clean, He can create you a new person!

He can make you—
"a house of prayer."

---

[9] James S. Stewart, "The Strong Name," Scribners, p. 67,68
[10] I Cor. 6:19 Phillips

CHAPTER 12

THE HUMBLE JESUS

"Behold, thy King cometh unto thee, meek" (Mt. 21:5)

We have always had a good time with Palm Sunday, haven't we? Here is our big moment in Christianity. Here for once we have something to crow about. Our King has come. He has entered the great city of Jerusalem, triumphantly, boldly, courageously, majestically. For once He showed them that He really is the King of Israel.

So, for one Sunday we can forget all about the humble, self-denying, quiet Jesus who goes about the countryside avoiding publicity. We can forget the serious, solemn notes of Christianity. We can forget the cross. Why should we think about the cross now? Jesus shows them who He really is! Jesus arrives as King. He is King of Kings and Lord of Lords. Is He not coming again as King? Is He not the Lord of all? Can we not sing the "Hallelujah Chorus," and for one Sunday in the year throw off all our self-restraint and have a good time? Isn't that the message of Palm Sunday? Your King comes! Hosanna! Rejoice!

Yes, I think even more than on that great, triumphant Sunday which follows Palm Sunday, we are happier now than on Easter. Easter is too close to Good Friday. With all the talk about resurrection, death still lurks ominously in the background. But not on Palm Sunday. All is royal.

Here is a fulfillment of prophecy: "Tell ye the daughter of Sion, Behold, thy King cometh unto thee, meek, and sitting upon an ass, and a colt the foal of an ass."[1]

An acclaim from the multitude: "Hosanna to the son of David: Blessed is he that cometh in the name of the Lord; Hosanna in the highest."[2]

An upset religious order: "Master, reprimand your disciples."[3]

A whole city clamoring with the question: "Who is this?"[4]

We have something to crow about. Who will deny this impact on the city? And yet, those people little understood what it was all about—in whose presence they were. Their answer to the question: "Who is this?" is shallow, indeed: "This is Jesus the prophet of Nazareth of Galilee."

No, this is the same Jesus who comes riding into Jerusalem, who has never sought publicity. He is not set on making a big splash. He has always avoided the reporters who could swarm like vultures upon any public figure.

[1]Mt. 21:5
[2]Mt. 21:9
[3]Lk. 19:39 English
[4]Mt. 21:11

He is the same Jesus who did not choose influential theologians or gifted preachers, but very ordinary fellows to be His apostles.

He is the same Jesus who never approached men of position or influence, the policy makers, the select intelligentsia, but who always hobnobs with the forgotten people by the side of life's road, the beggar, the leper, the outcast, the sinner—people who will never be considered important converts!

He is the same Jesus who teaches in simple words and homely stories, but never tries to impress anyone with big words.

He is the same Jesus who avoids crowds, shuns publicity, and withdraws into remote places for prayer.

He is the same Jesus who was born in a barn, lived in a small town, worked as a carpenter, and knelt in an upper room to wash His disciples' dirty feet.

He is the same Jesus who now enters Jerusalem in the fulfillment of that ancient prophecy. It takes courage to come so dramatically and boldly, to spell out this prophecy and demonstrate it before the people. But we have overlooked one word: "Thy King cometh unto thee, *meek, ...*"[5]

He enters humbly on a donkey. The heroes of the world come on horses. They are men of power. He comes on a beast of burden, symbolizing peace. The proud rulers of the world are surrounded by weapons of war. Jesus has only palm branches around Him. Most rulers come well protected by police and

---
[5]Mt. 21:5

142

secret service men. He arrives unprotected. He comes humbly. And when the parade peters out and the shouting dies down, He seems to slip away. He gets lost among the temple crowd.

Humility has marked Him from birth. We cannot avoid it at any time in Jesus' life. Therefore, the portrait of the humble Christ is particularly on exhibit on Palm Sunday. Palm Sunday cannot be an empty carefree celebration, completely out of character from everything else we have seen in Him.

Jesus is not a nationalistic deliverer. He is not another Jewish King. He is not going to enforce His rule on anybody. He has nothing to say about military Rome or Israeli triumph. His message is righteousness and peace.

When He returns as King, He is still the same Jesus. Were not the disciples told when He ascended to heaven, "This same Jesus, which is taken up from you into heaven, shall so come in like manner as ye have seen him go . . . ?"[6] He is the same. He will not be changed. His rule is righteousness. His Kingdom peace. He obtains His victory by the sword which comes from His mouth. No other sword: "Out of his mouth goeth a sharp sword, that with it He should smite the nations."[7] That sword is His gospel. This is how He conquers the world.

Do not divorce this triumphant entry from all else we know of Jesus. He is the same Jesus who comes humbly. We cannot forget the Cross at any time. We behold the portrait of the humble Christ.

God never did make a fuss about Himself! There

---

[6]Acts 1:11
[7]Rev. 19:15

is, of course, that miraculous journey through the Red Sea. There is thunder and lightning from Mt. Sinai. But when you think of it, these great miraculous events are few in the long history of the world. God comes so quietly to Abraham and promises him a son; hardly a world-shattering event. God makes Himself known to Elijah by a still, small voice. Who else really has time to listen? God comes to a shepherd tending sheep and lays His hand on his shoulder. That is how Amos becomes a prophet.

All this makes Him so hard for us to find! He calls no attention to Himself with a voice blaring from heaven over a celestial loudspeaker. God announces Himself to a teenage girl, is born as a little baby, and hardly anybody pays attention. He begins helping nobodies in the forgotten part of an all but forgotten country in a small corner of the Roman Empire. He has time for women and children, and lays His hands on miserable people who live in dirty places. He arrives, telling us that God's kingdom is like a hidden treasure. He who wants God will have to go looking. God makes no fuss about Himself.

Jesus does not come marching down the avenue with bands playing, flags flying, clothed in kingly purple, waving to the jubilant crowd. He does not come marching in front of legions of angels to impress us with His strength. Why not? Why should He not overwhelm this world a little? Why should He not display the power of God and give us something to believe in?

Because, then, we can only admire Him in the crowd. We can only wave to Him. We can never get close to Him. Because, what we really want is to be recognized. We want to get close to Him. We do not want to be lost in a crowd. We are so very much alone. We stand "alone in the rain." And no one seems to know that about us. No one seems to care. If Jesus comes striding through the world as some Messianic King, what good is that for me? That's not what I need!

How then do I see this humble Christ? He helps one beggar, one leper, one Mary Magdalene, one Nicodemus. He comes near to us. He tells us that this God who is, indeed, hidden is not playing hide-and-seek. He is near. He is in Jesus. He humbles Himself, takes on human flesh, and even humiliates Himself on a cross. We can find God if we want to. We can find Him before this supreme humiliation. We can find God on a cross!

In all His revelation of God, in His submission to death, and in everything He does as a Man, Jesus is meek. The hosannas of Palm Sunday are but the outer wrapping, which when removed, reveal the inner spirit of our King. And the crowd which for the moment is carried along with all this excitement returns to its old stupidities because it has not penetrated the meaning of this triumphal entry. The humble God of the universe upon a donkey! "Thy King cometh—meek."

I cannot for a moment agree with Nietzsche that "pity is a paralyzing mental luxury, a waste of feeling for the irredeemably botched, the incompetent, the defective, the vicious . . . "[8] I could probably worship a God who remains aloof, afar off, who is a

---

[8]Quoted from Will Durant on F. Nietzsche, "The Story of Philosophy," Simon and Schuster, p. 315

King in a triumphant procession. But I can far more worship a God Who becomes man for man's salvation. The pity of God for man is the essence of our salvation.

Why are we drawn to Jesus? Is it not this humility, this unpretentiousness, this divine pity for fallen man? Other religious figures seem to put on a theatrical exhibition. They pray, fast, and give to impress the crowd. He can honestly say, "Come unto Me, all ye that labor . . . for I am meek and lowly in heart."[9] And we believe Him. His life reveals it. He *is* meek and lowly in heart.

He shows utter humility at the end of His life. He submits. "He is brought as a lamb to the slaughter, and as a sheep before her shearers is dumb, so He openeth not his mouth."[10] God Himself goes this far!

This is not weakness. Jesus does not submit because He has no other way out. "Don't you realize that I could appeal to my Father, and He would at once send more than twelve legions of angels to defend Me?"[11] He said just prior to the Cross. To equate Jesus' action with defeatism or spineless resignation is to misunderstand humility. "I have power to lay (my life) down, and I have power to take it again."[12] The cross spells our salvation because of the complete humiliation of God's Son.

I even catch this humility in Jesus' resurrection. He does not parade before Pilate, Herod, Caiaphas

[9]Mt. 11:28,29
[10]Isa. 53:7
[11]Mt. 26:53 Phillips
[12]Jn. 10:18

and company. He could very well have gone back to the temple to stun the multitudes, or silence the skeptics. No such tactics. His appearances to the disciples could have been announced by heavenly trumpeters and performed with all the impressive splendor of a victorious king. Instead, He comes to them quietly at breakfast or dinner time. He joins a couple on a trip. He meets Peter in the lonely, tragic moments after his denial. He is the same Jesus, meek and lowly in heart. "Behold your *King*—meek."

Does not this Christ who comes so humbly tell us something about our manhood? We are agreed on the virtues of humility. We agree, too, that we ought to be humble. We do not like people whose only topic of conversation seems to be themselves. But have we ever seen in the portrait of the humble Christ, that Jesus, who really is somebody, goes around like a nobody? That Jesus who really is King never draws attention to Himself? That Jesus who really is God becomes fully and humbly—man? He really has something to crow about, but He never does.

This should tell us something about ourselves. We are quick to admit our limitations about things we don't understand. I am very humble about my knowledge of electronics, ballistics, or the workings of the stock market. The reason is simple. I know next to nothing about them. But, I am not so humble about my theological grasp. I know something about the Bible. The temptation is to let others know, I know. It is hard to be humble in this field. And yet precisely here, in this speciality I have—whether it's cooking, crooning, or computing—I must learn to be humble.

Jesus never tries to impress anyone with Himself. He is somebody. He is the King. He knows the truth. But He does not blow a trumpet before Him. Why is He so completely humble? Because He knows man's fleeting, shadowy existence. He knows our limitations. He only points men to God. He is humble as a man.

Small wonder then, that humility is a qualification to enter the kingdom.

"Humble we must be if to heaven we go,
  High is the roof there, but the gate is low."[13]

"Whosoever therefore shall humble himself as this little child, the same is greatest in the kingdom of heaven."[14]

This is no mere entrance requirement. It is an invitation for life! The more we draw near to God, the less we think of ourselves. The more we concentrate on His glory, the less we will consider our "greatness." The more we turn to Jesus, the nearer we are to the gospel. The more we grow in humility, the more we will realize the cross really is for us.

Here then are two ways to become humble: (1) Think of God. Draw near to Christ. Meditate on the cross. (2) Consider your own limits, the frailty of man. Meditate on the unassuming character of Jesus.

But, if we really want to be humble, there is only one other way open—the way of humiliation. He who would be humble must be willing to be humiliated. Here we balk. We want God on our own terms.

---

[13]Author Unknown
[14]Mt. 18:4

We want God to approve us as we are. Humiliating experiences are not for us. Everyone of us has more than one story tucked away which begins with the words, "I was never so humiliated in my life . . . "

God does not want to embarrass you before people. He does not cherish your humiliating experiences. I cannot conceive of God like that. But His purpose in these experiences is that they don't "get" you, that you really become humble. Humiliation must not upset you. The reason why Jesus did not go around with a story, "I was never so humiliated in my life . . . " is obvious: He *was* humble. Nothing could touch Him. Jesus was humiliated by what they said to Him and did to Him, publicly, openly, and finally, shamefully at Calvary. "We hid as it were our faces from him; He was despised, and we esteemed him not."[15] He could stand it to be humiliated.

The chief mark of a Christian is humility. But we are not saints, we confess to ourselves, and don't expect to be. God is holy, but we are not. Christ is humble. We are far from it. We admire the ideal. But we consider reaching it unattainable. Our conduct lags behind our creed. We go around with a cloud of hopelessness hanging overhead.

But, don't you see, as long as we think of humility as an ideal, beautiful but unattainable, that we will never even try for it? Don't you see that even with all our theology about Christ saving us, if we flinch under every humiliation, and fail to see God's hand upon us, we will never be what we can be? The first

[15]Isa. 53:3

mark of a Christian is humility. It is not easy to reach. It was not easy for Jesus. Don't think it was! He prayed and struggled. He was tempted like us.

"God . . . . gives humility," says Thomas Kelly. "Growth in humility is a measure of our growth in the habit of the Godward-directed mind. And he only is near to God who is exceedingly humble . . . There is a humility that is in God Himself. Be ye humble as God is humble."[16] God gives humility to us.

And what does it mean to believe that Christ saves us and is in us? What does it mean to have Christ in us during the thick of our earthly struggle? Does it not mean victory, power, strength? Does nothing happen to a person who is a Christian? Is there no hope of progress toward the goal? Something should be happening, daily, continually, when we are born *anew*.

So—humility comes by considering the grandeur of God and the miserable limitations of man. Humility comes through humiliation. Humility comes by looking at the portrait of the humble Christ: "I am meek and lowly in heart." Not the show and not the shouting, but *"thy King—meek . . . ." That* is really our big moment in Christianity.

[16]Thomas Kelly, "A Statement of Devotion," Harper, p. 63

CHAPTER 13

THE CRUCIFIED JESUS

"And sitting down they watched him there" (Mt. 27:36)

Few themes, if any, have so occupied the artists in the Christian era as the crucifixion of Christ. No museum could house all the art of the Cross. The crucified Christ draws all men to Himself. Thackeray was one day walking on a road near Edinburgh with three friends. They passed a quarry and saw outlined against the sky a great wooden crane—like a cross. The novelist, who was by no means deeply spiritual, stopped, pointed, and murmured, "Calvary." They moved on silently, pondering, brooding.

But why? Why should this cross so capture our attention? Crucifixions there have been many. What makes James Russell Lowell pen these words:

"The Cross, bold type of shame to homage turned,

Of an unfinished life that sways the world,

Shall tower as sovereign emblem over all."[1]

Is there something unique about this crucifixion?

Surely, one of the reasons why this cross has caught our world by surprise is because of the Man

---

[1] James Dalton Morrison, "Masterpieces of Religious Verse," p. 190

who hung there. Even those who may not know very much about Jesus, who never expect to give Him more thought or time, will say, 'He was a good man; a kindly, virtuous, friendly man.' They explain the cross in this manner:

"What happened to Him generally happens to good people. They are misunderstood. They are not appreciated. They are 'crucified' in one way or another. It was a shame He was only thirty-three. He was so young! He had so many possibilities—such a future before Him!"

Mario Lanza had a voice like Caruso, but he could not control himself. Some said his chief temptation was overeating. For whatever cause, Lanza died at thirty-eight. The sentiment most frequently expressed concerning him was, "What a shame. He was *only* thirty-eight."

Jesus was so young. He was a good man with such a promising future. And what a great teacher He was! He held thousands spellbound with His stories. Is there a sermon anywhere in literature like unto the Sermon on the Mount? Undoubtedly the goodness and the greatness of this Man have captured the artists of the world.

And yet there is something else about Jesus that intrigues the thoughtful, His God-likeness. The young Greek dramatists employed a clever device. When their characters were entangled in a difficult situation, they introduced a god to save the hero and set him free. Horace counselled against "gimmicks." A god, said he, should only be introduced in tragedy to untie a knot that baffled all human skill.

Our human situation is like a Gordian knot. No

Alexander can slash it. Only God can untie it. The one and only God, incredible as this may seem, enters the world in Jesus Christ. He reveals life as it ought to be lived. He allows the forces of evil to close in on him. He suffers Himself to be killed. No celestial rescue party arrives to save Him at the last minute. God comes to save His people entangled in tragedy. God comes to extricate man. *This* makes the cross singular.

Count Bernadotte had been appointed mediator in an extremely tense Israel-Arab crisis. He asked Ralph Bunche of the United Nations what he was to do.

"Mediate peace between two fighting nations."

"Is that all I do?"

"Yes."

"How?"

"You can use only what you have," said Mr. Bunche, "your bare hands."[2]

Count Bernadotte did bring an armistice between Israel and the Arab world. But in the process the mediator gave his life. He was shot.

Jesus is the Mediator between God and man. He is God-become-Man for the purpose of mediation. He unties the tragic knot with His bare hands. He brings peace through His cross. Surely this fact grips the imagination of the artist. Who dies on the cross? A good man; a great man; a God-like man; the God-Man.

Are we not drawn to this crucified Christ because the death itself is ghastly? The horror, the torture,

---

[2]As told by Ralph Bunche in a television interview

the agony are beyond words. The gospel writers set down the facts in stark simplicity. Artists have attempted to recapture more of the details of a Roman crucifixion.

The procession marches to the place of execution with the criminal placed in the center of four Roman soldiers. A herald walks in front with the charge printed in black so all can read: "This is Jesus the King of the Jews."[3] The criminal is taken by the longest possible route through busy streets. He serves as a warning that "crime does not pay." While He carries His cross, He is lashed and goaded.

At the place of crucifixion the criminal is laid on top of the Cross, which lies flat on the ground. He is stripped naked except for a loin cloth. He is offered a medicated wine to dull the pain. (Jesus refused this drug.) Halfway up the upright beam is a small projecting ledge on which the body can rest, or else the nails in the hands will tear clean through. The nails are driven through hands and feet. Then the cross with the criminal on it is lifted up.

He hangs there, perhaps seven to nine feet above the ground. He can clearly see the soldiers gambling for His coat. He has no difficulty hearing the taunting remarks: "He saved others; himself he cannot save. If He be the King of Israel, let him now come down from the cross, and we will believe him."[4]

His unnatural position makes every movement a pain. It hinders the circulation of blood. The nails driven through the most sensitive part of the hands are torturous, and the wounds quickly inflame. A

---

[3]Mt. 27:37
[4]Mt. 27:42

burning thirst increases the agony, as death lingers. No vital organ is affected, so death comes tardy. Nevertheless in this physical agony, Jesus finds time and strength to speak to His mother, a disciple, a thief and—God.

At noon the sun refuses to shine. A terrifying darkness hangs over the city. By three the end is near. Jesus bows His head, letting it fall on His chest peacefully. The physical death is ghastly . . .

But does not spiritual suffering hold yet more sway over us? How can we ever plumb the depths of Jesus' thought? He dies for a world that crucifies Him? How does He feel hanging there rejected while those He healed and helped maintain a cold, indifferent silence and refuse to come to His aid? What thoughts enter the heart during this agony, while His close friends deny, betray, and utterly forsake Him?

He dies to save a world that does not want to be saved. He forgives sins that few want forgiven. He brings a peace that will be continually abused. He assumes a load that crushed Him, but who cares? Who notices? "He is despised and rejected of men; a man of sorrows, and acquainted with grief: *and we hid as it were our faces from him*."[5]

Is there any sorrow like unto His sorrow?
"Hard it is, very hard,
To travel up the slow and stony road
To Calvary, to redeem mankind; far better
To make but one resplendent miracle,
Lean through the cloud, lift the right hand of power

---

[5] Isa. 53:3

And with a sudden lightning smite the world
   perfect.

Yet this was not God's way, Who had the pow-
   er,
But set it by, choosing the cross, the thorn,
The sorrowful wounds. Something there is, per-
   haps,
That power destroys in passing, something
   supreme,
To whose great value in the eyes of God
That cross, that thorn, and those five wounds
   bear witness."[6]

                (Dorothy Sayers)

Love suffers. This makes it so meaningful. Love is
vulnerable. Love bears all things. God does not look
out for number one. God is not concerned with security. God does not calculate and say, "Careful
now, this may lead me into suffering." He lays His
glory aside. He enters the world of sweat and tears.
He allows Himself to be trampled on.

"To love at all is to be vulnerable. Love anything,
and your heart will certainly be wrung and possibly
be broken. If you want to make sure of keeping it
intact, you must give your heart to no one. Wrap it
carefully round with hobbies and little luxuries;
avoid all entanglements; lock it up safe in the casket
or coffin of your selfishness." And in that casket of
selfishness your heart begins to change. It becomes
hard, unbreakable, irredeemable. "The only place
outside Heaven where you can be perfectly safe from
all the dangers of love is Hell."[7]

[6]James D. Morrison, "Masterpieces of Religious Verse," p. 189
[7]C. S. Lewis, "The Four Loves," Harcourt, Brace & Co., p. 169

God is not safe in hell. Some would classify "God" there—stoic, aloof, detached, disinterested in His creation, outside the human predicament, safe from all the dangers of love. This is far from the Christian gospel. Jesus loves with all the consequences of tragedy. The cross spells out this suffering love.

Daniel T. Niles gives us a penetrating illustration. The Hindu temple, he says, is built in the form of a man. The outer court is the human body. The inner court is the mind. The shrine is man's soul. Man moves inside himself to find God.

The Moslem mosque is built in the form of a man. The central dome is man's head. The minarets are hands upraised in prayer. Man comes to God through prayer.

The Buddhist dagoba is built in the form of a man. The erect body, the legs crossed, the head unmoving symbolize withdrawal from the world. Man reaches God through meditation.

The Christian Church is built in the form of a man. The man is on the cross. All traditional Church architecture, Romanesque, Gothic, even Byzantine, is based on a cross. All worship centers in that cross, the place where God and man meet. Man, therefore, approaches God through One who died.[8]

To the Hindu, Moslem and Buddhist, God is removed from the human scene. He is approached through meditation, prayer and quietness. To the Christian, God is touched with our infirmities. God knows the meaning of suffering. God experiences the

---

[8] D. T. Niles, "Upon The Earth," McGraw-Hill, p. 100-101

cross. He is not far away. He is there. He is found at the cross.

As difficult as it may be to think of a suffering God, we dare not shrink from our pursuit. A father's hair turns grey because of the sins of his son. A mother feels the stab in her heart, because her children reject her counsel. Is it wrong to get involved? Does not our Father in heaven allow Himself to feel? He does. He sends His Son. He suffers, too. There is a cross down here. There is a cross up there! We can never fully understand, but we can get involved by faith! The cross is the place where God meets man.

Is the penetrating artist not also intrigued by the fact that Jesus goes to that cross open-eyed? He wants to. He knows why He has come to earth. He will drink the cup of suffering to the bitter end. The cross is the result of a love that will not shrink, a love that will not leave men alone. He can ignore this blasphemous world, but He will not. He loves the world, and the price of love is death. On the cross sin worked its worst. Love worked its best. Sin was defeated, because love was triumphant.

Why was this all necessary? "Christ died for our sins."[9] Jesus does something for us which we cannot do for ourselves. Could we have done it for ourselves, the cross would be superfluous. The fact is we have lost paradise. We cannot just return.

"In preaching the gospel, the main appeal is to be made to the conscience ... it cannot be made too soon, too urgently, too desperately, or too hopefully . . . The Atonement is addressed to the sense of sin.

---
[9] I Cor. 15:3

It presupposes the bad conscience. Where there is no such thing, it is like a lever without a fulcrum; great as its power might be, it is actually powerless . . ."[10]

Jesus has come to do something in behalf of our sins. "If man had not sinned, the Son of Man would not have come," said Augustine.

He knows no sin, yet He enters the experience of carrying our sins. No illustration can compare with this truth, but perhaps it can illuminate. During World War I the English were greatly disturbed by a trench fever that affected the soldiers. They thought lice spread the disease. They sent for Bacot, a scientist, who had made a study of lice. Bacot took the lice, put them in small pill boxes and attached them to his lower arms. He went about his work, receiving hundreds of bites a day. He travelled to the various scenes of battle helping the soldiers. Constantly he tested cures on himself. Finally he became completely infected with typhus and died. He who was clean became unclean to save others.

Is not this the love of Jesus which has captured the world? He has died for us at infinite cost. He has done what we could not do. He has borne our sins. He has assumed a responsibility we could never assume. He who was clean became unclean in death for us.

"And sitting down, they watched Him there,
 The soldiers did;
 There, while they played with dice,
 He made His sacrifice,
 And died upon the Cross to rid

[10]James Denney, "The Death of Christ" Hodder & Stoughton, p. 219,220

God's world of sin.

He was a gambler, too, my Christ,
He took His life and threw
It for a world redeemed.
And ere His agony was done,
Before the westering sun went down,
Crowning that day with crimson crown,
He knew that He had won."

(G. Studdert-Kennedy)[11]

He has won, if He has won you. Everyone of us must face that cross. Everyone of us needs to come personally. "He died for me." Put the "me" into it. Only when you begin there, will the love of Christ begin to dawn in you.

Here is the height to which the Christian artist climbs. *This* meaning of the cross captures his heart! The goodness and greatness of Jesus ... He is the God-Man. His physical suffering and spiritual agony are for the world—for me. He "loved me, and gave himself for me."[12]

[11]James D. Morrison, "Masterpieces of Religious Verse," p. 187
[12]Gal. 2:20

CHAPTER 14

THE LIVING JESUS

"I am the resurrection and the life . . ."
(Jn. 11:25)

"I give unto them eternal life . . ."
(Jn. 10:28)

Most of us have the idea that what the Church is really about is religion. We go to Church to add a little bit of God to our overall lives. We put a little goodness into the glove compartment marked, 'religion', while the stationwagon of our lives barrels down the highway full of many other interests.

As long as you think of Christianity as 'religion' it is very easy to forget it. A car runs fine without a glove compartment. Religion is for those who want to be religious, but it is not necessary on life's road. Religion is a page in *Time* or *Newsweek* or the Saturday paper, which you can skip, because you couldn't be less interested. Religion is an occasional radio or television program religious people listen to, but you may as well turn to another channel. You go to Church when you feel like going. Most of the time you don't feel like going. Why go to Church when you can just as well stay home and read a good book or the Sunday paper or catch up on your gardening or enjoy a ballgame, or. . .? You have so little time to yourself anyway.

164

And so it becomes easy to dismiss religion as a force in today's world. After a brilliant survey of the literature of Western man, J. B. Priestley writes his penetrating conclusion that religion cannot save the world. Then he confesses: "I have no religion; most of my friends have no religion; very few of the major modern writers we have been considering have had any religion; and what is certain is that our society has none."[1]

Even if you are not as radical as that, you may end like the old salt, who after a couple of drinks told his theologian friend; "I too believe in God, and in the evening when the sun goes down, I always say to it, 'I hope you come up safely again.' That's my religion."[2] Not much religion!

Now I want a truth to strike you with all the blast of an air-raid siren while you're standing on the street corner directly under it—and least expect it. Jesus never mentioned "religion." Jesus never said a word about "religion." Jesus said nothing about putting a little bit of God in a certain compartment. He did say (in effect) that God should be at the wheel.

Jesus spoke about Truth and Light and Life. He does not bring us religion but life, "and that ... more abundantly."[3] He offers no religious additions to life, but life itself. Not a page in *Time* but all of Time belongs to God. Jesus does not call us to new religion but to new life; life so revolutionary and radical that He can only describe it as death to the

[1] J. B. Priestly, "Literature and Western Man", Harper, p. 445
[2] Helmut Thielecke, "Voyage to The Far East", Muhlenberg, p. 119
[3] Jn. 10:10

old and birth to the new. "You must not be surprised that I told you that men must be born again."[4]

You can dismiss religion but not life. Jesus says: "I am the resurrection and the life."[5] Here it hangs in the most honored place in our gallery, the portrait of the Living Christ, the featured attraction. Look closely and you will see that Christ is life, and Christ gives life.

"We know life and death only through Jesus Christ. Outside of Jesus Christ, we know neither what our life is, nor our death, nor God, nor ourselves," said Pascal.[6] If this is true, then those who do not know Christ do not know or have life. And that is exactly what the Bible says: "Any man who has genuine contact with Christ has this life; and if he has not, then he does not possess this life at all."[7]

"But that is ridiculous," you say, "I may not be a very religious person, but I'm alive. I'm just as alive as Jesus was. I have life, too!"

Of course you do. But what does Jesus mean by "life?" What do you mean by it? We speak of plant life, animal life and human life. We use the same word to describe all three. Do you mean by life that you have feeling, emotions, desires? Our pets have emotions and desires and hurt feelings, too. Do you mean by life the ability to have a family and raise children? The whole animal world knows the joy of reproduction from the tiniest guppies to the crocodiles in the zoo. To be a cog in the machine without

[4]Jn. 3:7
[5]Jn. 11:25
[6]Emile Cailliet, "Pascal, The Emergence of Genius", Harper, p. 333
[7]I Jn. 5:12 Phillips

any serious question, to follow the round of eating, sleeping, working, reproducing—this does not distinguish us from animal existence. This is not yet life.

Lawrence of Arabia was a world-famous leader. He succeeded in brilliant military victories and was idolized by the Arabs. Churchill called him one of the greatest hopes of the British empire. But after his exploits as a world-famous colonel, Lawrence enlisted as a common soldier in the RAF. Why? His life was empty. His work seemed meaningless. He felt like a failure. So he proceeded to make himself anonymous. He wanted to be merely a screw in the machine rather than the operator of the machine. This great leader of men went into hiding among the ranks.

We have done the same. We have allowed our great American way of life to squash us into becoming screws in a huge machinery. We have become a social security number, a credit card, a taxable object. We are one cog in the assembly line of democracy. We have allowed ourselves to be one of the millions who sit glued before the same monotonous television fare from Podunk to Wichita Falls to New York. Is this life? Is this what Jesus means by living?

But when you started to tell me that you have life just as Jesus has life, I caught something else in your voice. You were not so sure about it. You really meant to say:

"I have life now, yes, but I'll admit I have death, too. Death is always with me, chasing me. I cannot escape death! My whole life is a race against time. I'm in a hurry. I have no time. What's wrong with me? I'm alive but I never seem to have time . . . I live in a shadow of death."

There it is. Always mudding up our newly cleaned floors, following us, leaving its dirty footprints. I don't think we are conscious of death every minute. But whenever we turn around . . . then we start running again. We want to live!

We flit around from one diversion to another. We keep on the move following our instincts, yielding to our impulses, making money and making love, money and love, love and money. Religion is unimportant. Morals are old fashioned. God has no authority over us. "Let us eat and drink; for tomorrow we die."[8] Death will destroy it all—the life we live, the plans we make, the things we accumulate, the fun we are having. Death is the end. So final. So ruthless. Live it up now. Live before the clock runs down. Live while there is TIME . . . because we live in that horrible shadow.

But if there is nothing more to life than that—no meaning, no purpose, no knowledge of God or Christ—how pathetic life becomes. You had such hollow undertones in your voice when you said: "I have life, too!"

We believe in the importance of human life. Every doctor, nurse, druggist, ambulance driver, policeman, fireman, social service worker, psychologist, psychiatrist, etc., is dedicated to that task. Every time the ambulance rushes through our streets it is to preserve one human life. Some years ago a little girl fell down an abandoned well in Southern Cali-

[8]I Cor. 15:32

fornia. When she was discovered alive, they dangled a rope down, but she failed to tie herself to it. Then extensive rescue operations began. The problem was to get to the girl without the earth around caving in. Engineers gave of their learning, workmen of their time. With heavy equipment they labored around the clock for days. It was front-page stuff every day . . . world news all but forgotten. They finally reached her too late. All that concentration was on one life. Surely, it was not wrong.

Yet, why should she be saved? What should anyone be saved for? Why all the fuss in the hospitals to preserve this earthly existence? Is it because we realize that life is sacred? Is it because we know that we are more than bodies, that we are souls? Is it because instinctively we know, we are eternal? "Surely life is more than food."[10]

But Jesus comes to bring us life with no undertones of sadness, and no fear of death. "I am the resurrection and the life."[11]

His disciples heard that before His death. They were with Him every day. He knew the meaning of life. He lived without fear, without anxiety, without despair. But when He died it was all over. What availed it now that He drew so near to God and made God so real to them? He is dead. What good was it now to have known the meaning of life and to have lived so courageously? He is dead! "I am the resurrection and the life?" He is dead.

Then came Easter, and their funeral is turned into a festival! He is risen. He is alive. He is the way, the

[10]Mt. 6:25 English
[11]Jn. 11:25

truth, the life. Death cannot hold Him. He is victor. He is the resurrection. He is triumphant over death. "I am alive forevermore ... and have the keys of hell and of death!"[12]

(We do not now need to examine the authenticity of the resurrection. No doubt it occurred, or Christianity is built on a lie, and all our hopes crumble back into dust. Then there is no meaning to life whatsoever. If there had been no resurrection the Christian church would never have come into being.)

Why should we live on the wrong side of Easter? We can know Him who is alive. We may have this life with all its meaning. Life without disillusion, without defeat, without death dogging our every step. "Any man who has genuine contact with Christ has this life."

All who have not run away from death but have stared it in the face, who know life through Christ and have honestly searched out the meaning of this earthly existence can live above fear. Christ removes our fears. And when death loses its terror, time is no longer an enemy. When you know Christ you know life is forever. You don't have to run away. Now there is no point to live merely as a social security number, for love and money, a screw in the machine, or as one of millions condemned to the same monotonous entertainment.

"To me to live is Christ,"[13] said Paul. That is the meaning of life. "And to die is gain!" That is the removal of the fear of death.

---

[12]Rev. 1:18
[13]Phil. 1:21

"Safe shall be my going," sang Rupert Brooke,
"Secretly armed against all death's endeavor;
Safe though all safety's lost; safe where men fall;
And if these poor limbs die, safest of all."

"But," you say, "this may be of interest, now please bring it down where I can understand it. You want me to be free from the fear of death. You want me to live so that I'm not running against the clock. You want me to find meaning in life so that I don't allow the entertainment masseurs to knead and mold me like dough. You want me to know Christ. But how? What must I do? How ca I live this way? How can I know Christ?"

This brings me to the other great truth in the portrait of the living Christ. He who IS life also GIVES life. He gives His life in death. He lays it down for us. In giving His life in our place, He substitutes Himself for us.

"The good shepherd lays down his life for the sheep. I am the good shepherd; I know my own sheep and my sheep know me . . . I lay down my life for the sheep. I give unto them eternal life."[14]

"Who ever paid for the death of another by his own except the Son of God?" asks Tertullian. This Christian doctrine of substitution should not be so difficult. We know how a human life can be saved by a blood transfusion, when blood from another is pumped into the dying man. We have already seen that we are dying, for all our days are spent under

[14]Jn. 10:11,14,15,28 English

the lengthening shadow of death. He dies for us. "It was no perishable stuff, like gold or silver, that bought your freedom . . . The price was paid in precious blood . . . the blood of Christ."[15]

If this illustration is too physical, consider that we can be changed by words and ideas. The sciences of psychology and psychiatry have made us aware that a patient can be helped not by drugs or medication but by the transfer of healthy ideas. The counsellor "saves" his patient by words. He gives of himself. So the risen Christ can give us faith and hope when we listen to His word or read the Bible.

This illustration falls short, too, for we are not saved by Christian ideas but by Christ. He comes into this world. He identifies Himself with us. He dies in our place. He rises from the dead. He re-enters heaven. He can save us because He is the living Christ. He can save us because He gives eternal life.

Obviously a gift can only be received. You cannot earn it. You cannot pay for it. You cannot buy it. You must take it. Jesus died for the whole world, but only those who receive Him become the children of God. Not every one who may vote, does. "It is by his grace you are saved, through trusting him; it is not your own doing. It is God's gift, not a reward for work done."[16]

We cannot *make* God gracious to us by anything we do. He *is* gracious. We cannot qualify for grace by an ethical life, for if some could, others could not. How then would they be saved? If only the good qualify, why does the Bible say He died for *all*? In

[15] I Peter 1:18,19 English
[16] Eph. 2:8,9 English.

fact, if the good can qualify, Jesus did not have to die for us. Either life is a gift, or else it is obtained by goodness.

What this really means is that everyone has a chance. Everyone can be saved. Even the vilest. Even the lowest. Even me, even you. We must become like little children to enter the kingdom of God. Little children never quibble about gifts. Whenever I offer mine a gift, they hold out their hands for it because they want it.

Why then go on living on the wrong side of Easter? Life is yours for the taking. You take it by faith, faith in the living Christ. You can't believe in a dead Christ. A dead Christ cannot give you life. A living Savior can. Eternal life—now and forever. "I give unto them eternal life." Take it. He offers it freely.

But now I must add one other truth which the Bible emphasizes. Christ is life and gives life to those who take it, but we must want it. We must mean it. We must be willing to keep knocking until the door opens. We must seek until we find. We must sell everything to buy the pearl of great price. We must hunger and thirst for righteousness until we are filled. We must be in earnest.

I am not saying we must work. I do not contradict the Biblical truth that life is a gift. But this is no gift for which you say "thank you" and then put away in a closet somewhere. This is not a gift you receive nonchalantly, almost as if you are doing the giver a favor. This is a very costly gift, a gift which cost God unimaginable pain and anguish; a gift which cost Jesus unbearable suffering and death.

Don't take it lightly. This gift is not for the reckless. It is not for those who play at religion. Only those who stake everything on this bottom card receive life. Only those who are driven to their knees in earnest and cry out, "God be merciful to me a sinner,"[17] obtain mercy.

Stuart Hamblen, former Hollywood playboy, tells the story of his conversion during the Billy Graham campaign in Los Angeles. After attending a few meetings he was under a deepening conviction. It all came to a boiling point one night at three thirty. In the middle of that sleepless night he called Billy Graham. The evangelist told him to come right over. As Hamblen walked in, the first thing he said was:

"Billy, let's pray."

"No, wait a minute."

Hamblen exploded: "Do you mean to tell me that you caused me all this hell, and then you are not going to pray with me?"

"No."

He was about to punch Billy in the mouth, he says, but calmed down and asked: "Why?"

"Stuart, I will not get on my knees with you until you promise to give up everything that is mean and vile and wicked in your heart."

"Let's pray, Billy."

"No. You've got to make that promise."

That was about the hardest thing he had ever done in his life! "Give up everything. . .?" All right . . . some things, yes, but everything? . . . not that, no,

---

[17]Lk. 18:13

not that one thing. Everything else, but not that . . .
all right, that too. . .

"OK, Billy," he said, "OK, I'll give them up."
Then they prayed. Then Christ entered.

Jesus comes to us when we really mean it. He can
come anytime. He is gracious and full of mercy, but
He comes when we are at the end of our rope.

Sometimes our Christianity resembles one of
God's creatures—the flying fish, very delightful to
watch. He lives in the sea, but he will make a brief
excursion into the air, glisten in the sun, attract the
glance of onlookers, and then dive back into the
water. On Easter Sunday (and sometimes every Sunday) we jump out of the sea around us, shine in our
churchly best, attract the admiration of all who take
notice, and then plop back into our native world.

God is not interested in flying fish exhibitions.
God is not impressed by Christianity on display. He
will not save a flying fish Christian who takes Christ
as lightly as that . . . God for a few seconds and then
forgets about Him? God is only found by those who
are in earnest.

Now we are back where we started. Flying fish
Christianity is like adding a little bit of God to our
overfull lives. It is merely religion. And religion is a
page in Saturday's press. You can dismiss it. Religion is for the religious. But not life. That's too
exciting! We want to live. Jesus offers us life, not
religion; a transformed life, a changed life, a new
life, brought about by the violence of new birth:
"You must not be surprised that I told you that men
must be born again."

Jesus does not care about our flying fish exhibition, when you come up for air to get a breath of religion. It's the sea around us in which He is really interested! Down there where you are in your native sea, in all that you do, in all that you are, in all that you think, in all that surrounds you week after week after week, He wants to give you *life*. That is what it means. Victory, joy, peace, forgiveness, love—*there where you live*.

"I am the resurrection and the life." Jesus is life.

"I give unto them eternal life." He offers life. Take His gift.

> I know you will—
> when you get desperate!

CHAPTER 15

THE KNOCKING JESUS

*"Behold, I stand at the door, and knock:
if any man hear my voice, and open
the door, I will come in to him, and
will sup with him, and he with me"
(Rev. 3:20)*

The question that really concerns all of us the most is the question "how?" Many of us sincerely believe the great truths of Christianity. But how can we live by them? This we want to know.

For example, many believe that Jesus is the Saviour of the world. But how does He save me? How does He become my Saviour? What does this mean? What must I do? That is my question, isn't it? I don't want objective facts. I need subjective experience.

The portrait of the knocking Christ hangs in the gallery to give us this answer. The more we look upon it, the clearer will be the reply to our questions: "Behold, I stand at the door, and knock: If any man hear My voice, and open the door, I will come in to him, and will sup with him, and he with Me."[1]

Originally Jesus said this to a church. It was a lukewarm, careless church, outwardly rich but inwardly poor, busy but empty. It was a prosperous

---

[1]Rev. 3:20

church and a flourishing one, but despite its religious preoccupation, blind to Jesus Christ, who stood *outside!*

That can be said of a man as well. Outwardly prosperous he may be inwardly poor; busy but empty, careless toward God, yet miserable in his heart. To such Jesus comes knocking. He stands outside.

And here is your first revelation as you look at this portrait of the knocking Christ. He creates the crisis! He precipitates the action. He takes the initiative. "Behold, I stand . . . and knock." You want to know how Jesus becomes your Saviour? That is not up to you in the first place. That is up to God. It has always been up to God! You don't start anything. Take the pressure off yourself. Jesus comes knocking. This is the good news.

The gospel is God's idea, not yours. God sent His Son into the world; He started it. Jesus came right down where we are; it was all His idea. Jesus died for our sins; He accomplished it. Jesus rose again from the dead; He triumphed. He stands at the door of our being because He is alive. He comes to us.

Do you see what we have here? We have the gospel, God taking on flesh, the crucifixion, the resurrection, without which Jesus cannot come to us. He cannot now come if He is not risen and alive.

He comes when He comes. We cannot force Him to come. It is entirely up to Him. I think we had better understand that. As long as we believe we can manipulate God or tell Him what to do and when He should do it, we are not acting as Christians. God is God.

There is such a thing as asking, but the answer depends on Him. There is a great need for us to seek, but finding is His business. He must reveal Himself. God comes pursuing us, Christ wants to find us, and the Holy Spirit woos us, but we cannot command Him. "Behold, I stand and knock." He comes when He comes. He initiates the action.

He knocks. We are so lukewarm toward God, so careless about heaven and so involved in earthly interests, that He *has* to come knocking at our life's door. If our salvation depended on us, no one would ever be saved. Still He does not force His way in. He will not break the door down. He could; but He is too much of a gentleman to force Himself on anyone. He is also too much of a Lover. He refuses to go away. . . .

Another insight will be yours as you gaze upon this knocking Christ. He Who creates the crisis also calls: "If any man hear My voice . . ." Apparently the knock is not enough. We have such a vague interest in God. We hear the knock and know someone is there, but fail to respond. Heaven's portals swing open at His command. Our doors remain closed. Therefore He calls. He stands and knocks and calls.

"If any man . . ." No one is excluded. No one needs to be lost. Jesus died for the world. Therefore He calls the world. This means He must come to every living person in some way at some time during life: Do not ask me how. That is God's business. I am only a servant in His Kingdom, but He is the Lord. I am only a child, and He is the Father who handles His own affairs.

You can be sure of this: You are not a headache to God. He does not condemn your past. What you have done and how much you have sinned is not His concern now. "Come now, and let us reason together, saith the Lord: though your sins be as scarlet, they shall be as white as snow."[2] He comes, is that not enough? He knocks, is that not assuring? He calls, what more do you want?

The voice clarifies the knock. The voice calls us to discipleship. The voice calls us to follow Him. But here is our dilemma. Do you hear anything? How do you hear God's voice? Can you hold a two-way conversation with God?

Let it be clear that the men of the Bible entered into conversation with God. Abraham discussed a city which had become a den of iniquity with God. Moses shared his fears, conscious of his inability to lead Israel out of Egypt. The prophets parried with God and pondered His answers. When God spoke, then they spoke.

More than any other, Elijah shared the secret of his conversation with God. He tells us how God speaks to him. He climbs a mountain and views the magnificent scenery below. A great wind violently rips into the mountain and breaks off some rocks, but God is not in the wind. A tremulous earthquake shakes the foundations, but Elijah cannot hear God in that quake. A fire breaks out in the valley below. God does not appear in the fire. And then, in the hush of the evening, Elijah hears "the still, small voice."[3]

[2] Isa. 1:18
[3] I Kings 19:11-13

"Often you should be silent and let Him speak," says Fenelon, "so that you may listen in the stillness of your heart."

God speaks when we listen. He speaks in prayer and worship and Scripture. He speaks in circumstance, dream, experience, conscience and every day occurrence. He speaks through voices of the past which give warning, offer rebuke, bring hope. He speaks until we change the subject. He speaks now: "Behold, I stand at the door, and knock: if any man hear My voice, and open the door. . ."

That brings us to the choice. He who creates the crisis and calls, offers us the choice. "If any man open the door . . ." He will not barge in. You have complete freedom. And He is gentle, persistent, loving.

What happens when someone comes to our door? We used to rush to find out who honored us with a call. We used to throw the door wide open and invite him in—even if he was a salesman. Not any more. So many people knock on our doors nowadays that we are extremely cautious. We call from an upstairs window, peep through a glass hole in the door especially made for that purpose, or at the boldest open the door a crack on the chain. We have been bitten by salesmen, and solicitors, crooks who take advantage of us.

No wonder we are cautious when Jesus comes. We may start a conversation from an upstairs window and are extremely reluctant to get near the door. Not children! They will run to the door any time the doorbell rings (unless adults have instructed them otherwise), throw it wide open and scream into the kitchen: "Mommy, it's a MAN." Must we not become like little children to receive Jesus?

We need not be cautious or afraid. God is not a supersalesman who must sell you His Kingdom. God is not a solicitor who needs your tithes. God is love. Christ is the Saviour of the world. He wants to forgive and cancel the past, so that you can face the future with confidence. He wants to enter and bring you love, peace, joy.

Are you apprehensive? You are not the first to fear the consequences. Listen to Augustine: "What I feared to be parted from, was now a joy to part with." He speaks for all who have made the great experiment and opened the door.

When Jesus knocks, the reply is up to you. Delay is dangerous. A Hindu doctor found Jesus and was willing to be baptized. He lived in a remote region which a Baptist minister only visited occasionally. Could baptism and public reception be postponed until the minister returned? Yes. That doctor is still a Hindu today. During the months preceding baptism his family brought pressure against him and he was never baptized. Can the harvest be lost? Perhaps!

The reverse is also true. Many have been baptized who are no longer serious Christians. They were baptized too soon under the pressure of a persuasive Christian. One can be too early or too late. But when Jesus knocks it is always the right time!

He stands. He knocks. He calls. It is for you to open the door. The familiar painting of Jesus knocking at the door is not great art. It has only this to commend itself, there is no latch on the door. The latch is on the inside. Jesus cannot open the door. Only you and I can.

Stop your divided uncertainties. Be done with your misery. Forsake that last fear. Put your hand on the doorknob. Remove the chain of doubt. Turn the handle and open up. If Jesus knocks and calls to you, this is the hour. The choice is yours.

The final truth in the portrait of the knocking Christ brings certainty. He creates the crisis: "Behold, I stand at the door, and knock." He calls: "If any man hear My voice." Yours is the choice: "Open the door." "I will come in to him, and will sup with him, and he with Me." All He needs is access. He wants to enter. He enters when the door opens.

But how can you know Jesus as your Saviour? How can you be sure? How can you know whether He has come in? That is the crux of the matter, isn't it? How can this certainty be mine? Now we tend to make this very complicated. It is not complicated.

Ask yourself, "Who speaks?" Jesus Christ.

"Can you believe Him?" Yes.

"Does He tell the truth?" Yes.

"Is this the Son of God who talks to me?" Yes.

"Then I will believe Him. If I open the door, He says He will come in. I believe Him."

Certainty comes through faith. Why does the Bible over and over again emphasize faith? Why are we constantly encouraged to believe God and His Word? Because only when we believe Him, will we let Him save us! If we believe in ourselves, God becomes a convenient addition to our self-confidence. If we do not trust in ourselves and know ourselves to be miserable, wretched and poor, then we will trust Him. This is what brought health and healing to the blind, the deaf, the lame, the lepers, and the sinful. They believed utterly. "Without faith it is impossible to please Him: for he that cometh to God must believe that He is, and that He is a rewarder of them that diligently seek Him."[4]

So, when we open the door of our heart to Him, we do not for a moment think there is no one there! When we open the door, *we do not face a vacuum.* Christ is there. He promises to enter. Certainty comes through faith, not mental gymnastics. We act on His Word. We commit ourselves to Him.

But there is far more than "mere faith." Jesus says: "I will come in . . . and will sup with him." He gives us an experience of Himself. When faith opens the door, joyful will be our experience. How does one experience Jesus? He is not here in the flesh.

Experience can be apart from physical form. You can be in a group of people and yet be attuned to another spirit. Christians have always testified to the "presence of Jesus." Quotations can be multiplied from apostles, saints, martyrs, missionaries and reformers. Each experience is personal, beginning in faith.

"He is where we are when we are attuned for His presence, as the music of another continent suddenly is where our radio set is . . . The mystery of this type of experience is no greater than the mystery of any other type of experience . . . It comes down in the last resort, to a question of *fact* . . . The taste of

[4]Heb. 11:6

sweetness, or the color-vision of redness, are just as unanalyzable and just as mysterious as is this instantaneous flash of God into our souls. We see stars billions of miles away, only because something from the star is actually operating on the retina and in the visual center of the brain; and so, too, we find God . . . in contact with the spiritual center within us that is kindred to Him."[5]

This experience can be for every day, all our lives long! Jesus says so: "I will sup with him and he with Me." Now the figure of speech takes a sudden turn. He who comes as guest is now host. We are guests at His table. He is Lord—He will only be Lord in our lives.

By this, too, we know the certainty of His presence. Not in our weakness, for we cannot accomplish one good thing in our flesh, but by His victorious power, by His triumphant adequacy, by His grip on our sanity and will, which is the result of His Lordship. He makes our experience incontrovertibly our own. No abstractions now. No vague mysticism. No romantic notions. No fancy speculation, but certainty: "This is what God has done and is doing for me." "We speak that we do know, and testify that we have seen."[6] "I know whom I have believed."[7] It remains only to act on what we know, and to act now.

How does Jesus become my Saviour? He creates the crisis. He calls. Mine is the choice. Certainty

[5]Rufus M. Jones as quoted by Thomas S. Kepler, "The Fellowship of The Saints," Abingdon-Cokesbury, p. 658
[6]Jn. 3:11
[7]2 Tim. 1:12

follows. I remember the young couple who came to talk to me after an evangelistic service. They had been going together for some time and were planning to be engaged; yet this was not foremost on their young minds that night. They were brought up in Christian homes. They had received the witness of Christian parents, teachers and friends. They believed Jesus was the Saviour of the world, but they did not know Him as their Saviour.

We talked about faith and certainty and about the knocking Christ. Then the ninteen-year-old boy and his eighteen-year-old girlfriend knelt in simple prayer, as they had often done before. Now their prayers were direct, humble, believing. When they rose from their knees, we talked again quietly, happily. An assurance had come from the living Lord. He was no longer merely the Saviour of the world. He was their Saviour and they knew it. They had simply taken Him at His Word.

"Behold, I stand at the door, and knock: if any man hear My voice, and open the door, I will come in to him, and will sup with him, and he with Me." Crisis, call, choice—certainty.

You can be too early or too late.

But if Jesus knocks,
now is the right time.

CHAPTER 16

THE COMPELLING JESUS

"Go ye therefore . . ." (Mt. 28:19)

The final chapter of a book states the conclusion. The end of a mystery reveals its solution. A play reaches its climax just prior to the curtain's fall. And so the final portrait of this exhibit of the portraits of Christ must reveal the purpose of this showing. What has been the meaning of it all? This portrait of the compelling Christ will answer that question.

All evangelists paint it.* They all emphasize the last week of Jesus' life. They begin with the triumphal entry, follow Him in His teaching, His suffering and trial, His death and burial. Then comes the trumpet note of resurrection, various appearances to believers, and finally the climactic portrait of the compelling Christ:

"All power is given unto Me in heaven and in earth. . . ." (Matthew)[1]

---

*I am aware that the ending of Mark's gospel (Mark 16:9-20) is not in some early manuscripts. Nevertheless, it *is* an ending and even a possible one. The original ending which was "lost" may have contained similar material to what we now possess in the other gospels.
[1]Mt. 28:18

"Go ye into all the world and preach the gospel to every creature. . . ." (Mark)[2]

"Repentance bringing the forgiveness of sins is to be proclaimed to all nations. . . ." (Luke)[3]

"As my Father hath sent Me, even so send I you." (John)[4]

The gospel which began, "Come and see", ends: "Go and preach."

The compelling Christ reveals the purpose of the incarnation. He compels us: "Go ye therefore, and teach all nations, baptizing them in the name of the Father, and of the Son, and of the Holy Ghost: Teaching them to observe all things whatsoever I have commanded you: and, lo, I am with you alway, even unto the end of the world."[5]

But it must strike you immediately that this missionary command is not only imperialistic but impertinent. Go to all nations? These nations have produced an Aristotle and Plato, a Seneca and Marcus Aurelius, a Zoroaster and Mohammed, a Confucius and Laotze, Krishna and Buddha. Go and tell them about Jesus? Baptize them in the name of the Father, the Son, and the Holy Spirit? All the evangelists agree. This is the finale. This is Jesus' concluding message.

What impertinent fanaticism, what self-flattering superiority, what religious intolerance! View this portrait and you must come to the conclusion that either Jesus is an arrogant fanatic, or He is the Saviour of

[2]Mk. 16:15
[3]Lk. 24:47 English
[4]Jn. 20:21
[5]Mt. 28:19,20

the world. If *God* entered the world in a third-rate country of the Roman empire, lived as a carpenter, died on a cross, and rose from the dead, this truth cannot remain in the backwoods. Jesus is either a bigot or He is the risen Lord who must be proclaimed as the world's only hope. You are driven to that either/or.

There is a desire among many intellectuals to fuse the best elements of the world's religions into one modern, all-inclusive, ethical religion. Remove all that is magic and miraculous, superstitious and supernatural, pool the ideas of the great teachers, and so bring harmony to the world. Find common ground in the ethical precepts of all religions.

But what has happened here? We decide what to keep and what to reject. We judge. Syncretistic religion is a religion of man's own making. It is ethical humanism whose horizon is this world. Therefore it cannot be of divine origin. And if "God" is brought into this super amalgamation, it is a "God" which man has chosen, rather than God Who has chosen man and revealed Himself to man.

A woman had been married for many years and had no children. She was a Protestant, and she had prayed often to God for children. In desperation one day she went to a Roman Catholic shrine and besought the Virgin Mary for a child, but to no avail. Once more she tried at a Hindu shrine and made vows. She became pregnant and had a child. Now she came to her Protestant minister and asked him whether she should change her faith and become a Hindu. The minister had this to say: "If having or not having children is to decide the issue, it does not really matter what you do. You can choose to belong to any religion you like."[6]

What is the issue? That's the question. Has God acted in history? Is God uniquely in Jesus Christ? Is Jesus Christ the Saviour of the world? Then we do not choose a religion. Then God chooses us.

Obviously Jesus does not allow us the possibility of syncretism. If He is another teacher among teachers, yes. If He is another great man who points the way to the good life, of course. Create one religion for one world. But Jesus says to us: "All power is given unto Me in heaven and in earth." No teacher ever said anything like that. All power is His because He is the risen Lord. And because He is the risen Lord, He is the Saviour of the world. There is no Saviour but Jesus. There is no Lord but the risen Lord. There is no power but His!

Perhaps this will become clearer if we ask: What does He want taught? What is His gospel? What is the message of the compelling Christ?

Is the message the Ten Commandments and obedience to God? If it is—no point to tell this to the Jews. Moses has already brought the Ten Commandments and taught the importance of obedience to God. Jesus' message, therefore, cannot be the Ten Commandments.

Is the message that we must love our neighbor as ourselves? The whole world knows this, and Confucius in particular has emphasized the love of neighbor as man's highest duty. Ethics is not news. The world already knows that it ought to "be good."

---

[6]D. T. Niles, "Upon The Earth," McGraw-Hill, p. 120

Is the gospel then that man should pray, meditate, and enter into communion with God? Then why enter India? The Hindus have much to teach us about the art of meditation and control of body and mind. That cannot be the gospel either.

Is the message that men should believe in heaven and prepare for an after-life? If that is the gospel why preach to the Buddhists? Buddha led his disciples to strive for the end of suffering and so attain the bliss of Nirvana. Most of the world's civilizations have believed in an after-life.

Therefore this Christian message is something other than obedience to God, love of neighbor, the necessity of prayer and belief in heaven. The Christian gospel is the proclamation of God who loves the world and sends His only Son to save it. "I want to speak about the Gospel...." said Paul, "Christ died for our sins, as the Scriptures said He would; He was buried and rose again on the third day, again as the Scriptures foretold."[7] All who put their confidence in Him will be saved: "For God so loved the world, that He gave His only begotten Son, that whosoever believeth in Him, should not perish, but have everlasting life."[8]

Proclaim to the Jew: the long-awaited Messiah has arrived! He has come; He was rejected; He has risen from the dead. Come and your sins will be blotted out. You will receive His Holy Spirit.

Go to the Greek, Roman, African and Asiatic and proclaim: God loves the world! He who made the sun and moon and stars has visited *this* planet. He

[7] I Cor. 15:1-4 Phillips
[8] Jn. 3:16

has come and suffered. They put Him to death when He came, even to a criminal's death, but He suffered it willingly for us. That is how much God loves the world. . . .

Tell all who long for eternity and dream about heaven, the gospel provides assurance for such hope. Jesus has risen. He triumphed over death. He is alive forevermore, and says: "Because I am really alive, you will be alive, too."[9]

This is the message of the compelling Christ. Do you wonder why He wants it proclaimed? And is it any wonder that Christians of all centuries have refused to allow this gospel to be laid down alongside man's ethical systems or fused into one world religion? "Go ye therefore, and teach all nations, baptizing them in the name of the Father, and of the Son, and of the Holy Ghost."

Baptism is simply the response to the proclamation of God—the Father who cares, the Son who dies, the Spirit who changes men—but one God. Baptism is in the *name* of God. Receive the proclamation. Identify yourself with the Father, the Son and the Spirit. Take His name upon you. Baptism signifies you belong to Him.

After this initial response to the proclamation comes the teaching. The Christian faith cannot be taught until it has been proclaimed and accepted. Baptism precedes teaching. Another religion stands or falls on the acceptance of ideas. A teacher of a new religion exists only if people accept his teaching.

---

[9]Jn. 14:19 Phillips

When people no longer believe, the religion vanishes. The Gnostics came and the Gnostics went.

Christianity cannot be taught until it has been proclaimed. The proclamation is this: "Jesus is the Saviour of the world. There is none other." Whether you believe it or not, whether you accept it or not, truth is. Your belief cannot change the fact. Jesus is Lord. After proclamation and baptism the teaching begins.

This teaching is the gospel of the kingdom. "Teaching them to observe all things whatsoever I have commanded you." Grow in discipleship. Learn to follow Jesus. Live in the certainty of His promise: "Lo, I am with you alway, even unto the end...." Until the end the gospel and the teaching center in Jesus Christ and His power.

And now as I look again at this portrait of the compelling Christ, I see a multitude behind Him. They have heard His message. They are compelled to proclaim it. In the foreground are the disciples. They fulfill their Lord's command to witness to all nations. Andrew goes to Greece. Philip to Asia Minor. Matthew arrives in Ethiopia. Peter travels to Rome. Thomas to India. All lie buried in foreign soil, but James who was martyred in Jerusalem.

By the end of the first century, four hundred Christians had multiplied to one-half million. How was it possible? They were compelled Christians. They had not many professional evangelists. They were all evangelists. They had few great preachers. They were all witnesses. They had few foreign missionaries. They were all missionaries.

Throughout the years compelled Christians have

proclaimed Christ. There were dark days when the Church lost its vision. "To spread abroad the knowledge of the Gospel amongst barbarous and heathen nations seems to be highly preposterous. . . . to propagate abroad would be improper and absurd," was a resolution passed by the Scotch Church in 1796.[10] At that very moment, however, light came and modern missions began. Carey went to India, Morrison to China, Judson to Burma, Livingstone to Africa, and a host of compelled Christians have stepped into this unfinished portrait ever since. . . .

Not only those who proclaim Christ professionally are His witnesses, for Jesus says: "Go ye." That "ye" is all-inclusive. It is a command, not a choice. It is an order, not an option.

Jesus gives us no reason: "The heathen are lost, therefore you must go. The need is great and missionaries are needed all over the world." No! We are His disciples; we have taken His name upon us in baptism; we are identified with Him—therefore we must share Him. There is no alternative.

We have to get clear away from the idea that proclamation is in the hands of the clergy. It was never meant to be that way. "You are the light of the world."[11] Every Christian life and testimony must be seen.

The ordinary man thinks that Jesus was a good teacher and a good man with a message about brotherhood—and goodness. All he knows about Jesus he garners from an occasional newspaper article or

---

[10]Quoted from H. E. Fosdick, "The Meaning of Service", Association Press.
[11]Mt. 5:14

glimpses from a Christmas television special. "The time has come for the Church to restate boldly and unequivocally that the Way, the Truth and the Life have all been revealed, that the Kingdom is here already and that the battle in which there can be no neutrality is on. The bankruptcy of humanism without God should be ruthlessly exposed ... We proclaim not a myth but a historic fact, not an idealistic pattern of behavior, but an active, joyful way of living life."[12]

We dare not leave this in the hands of the clergy. Jesus never intended for us to. Every baptized Christian is a witness of that Name.

What will compel us then and make Christ compelling? When we recognize who He is, why He came, and what He has accomplished, we will learn the secret. Receive the good news of God. Stare—literally stare—long and hard at this portrait of the compelling Christ. "All power is given unto Me in heaven and in earth. Go ye therefore ... baptizing ... teaching ... and, lo, I am with you alway."

So, this is the end. Better yet, it is the end of the beginning. The end of Jesus' ministry marks the beginning of the Church's ministry. The end of Jesus' stay on earth is the beginning of the Holy Spirit's work on earth. What Jesus began, the Church continues. What Jesus completed, the Church proclaims. This portrait is the end of the beginning, but it is also the beginning of the end.

In Jesus the end has begun. They who heard Him are they "upon whom the ends of the world are

[12]J. B. Phillips, "God Our Contemporary," Macmillan, p. 123,124

come."[13] That end will come; the curtain will fall, when Jesus returns. But that end has begun now, for Jesus says that all power already belongs to Him!

So, step into the portrait of the compelling Christ. For when "this gospel . . . shall be preached in all the world . . . then shall the end come."[14]

This portrait is unfinished. . . .

. . . .Let us finish it. . . .

"Then shall the end come."

[13]I Cor. 10:11
[14]Mt. 24:14